**Costs La
Reports**

2009 Part 5

Note on Citation

Costs Law Reports should be cited as Costs LR,
e.g. *1-800 Flowers Inc* v *Phonenames Limited* [2001] 2 Costs LR 286.

Note that cases and paragraphs are also numbered to allow for easier online referencing. (Where possible, paragraph numbering from original transcripts will be maintained.) Using this method, paragraph one of the *1-800 Flowers Inc* v *Phonenames Limited* judgment would be cited as: *1-800 Flowers Inc* v *Phonenames Limited* [2001] Costs LR Case 21 at [1].

Also, where neutral citation numbers are given, the original transcript numbering has always been maintained, allowing the neutral citation method to be used. Using this method, paragraph two of *1-800 Flowers Inc* v *Phonenames Limited* would be cited as: *1-800 Flowers Inc* v *Phonenames Limited* [2001] EWCA Civ 721 at [2].

Costs Law Reports

2009 Part 6

Peter Rogers
LL B
Deputy Costs Judge of the Supreme Court

Michael Bacon
MA (Cantab), FALCD, MAE, QDR

Text © Michael Bacon and Peter Rogers 2010

Typography © Class Legal 2010

COPYRIGHT

All rights reserved. No part of this publication may be reproduced in any material form (including photocopying or storing it in any medium by electronic means and whether or not transiently or incidentally to some other use of this publication) without the written permission of the copyright holder except in accordance with the provisions of the Copyright, Designs and Patents Act 1988 or under the terms of a licence issued by the Copyright Licensing Agency www.cla.co.uk. Applications for the copyright owner's written permission to reproduce any part of this publication should be addressed to the publisher.

ASSERTION OF MORAL RIGHTS

The author/editor asserts his/her right as set out in ss 77 and 78 of the Copyright Designs and Patents Act 1988 to be identified as the author/editor of this work wherever it is published commercially and whenever any adaptation of this work is published or produced including any sound recordings or films made of or based upon this work.

DISCLAIMER

The information presented in this work is accurate and current to the best of the author's/editor's knowledge. The author/editor and publisher, however, make no guarantee as to, and assume no responsibility for, the correctness or sufficiency of such information or recommendation.

Class Legal
Owl House, Carr Farm, Cadney, BRIGG,
Lincolnshire, DN20 9HP, UK
Tel: 01652 652222 Fax: 01652 651050
DX 24360 Brigg
Email: Info@ClassLegal.com
Website: www.ClassLegal.com

Class Legal is an imprint of Class Publishing Ltd, a company registered in England No. 2993127. VAT No: GB 503 5208 87

Registered Office: 7 Melrose Terrace, London W6 7RL, UK

PRINTING HISTORY

First published 2010

ISBN 978 185959290 8 ISSN 1366-8617

A CIP Catalogue for this book is available from the British Library

Typeset by: Stephen Theaker

Printed and bound by: Good News Press

Contents

Table of Cases   *vii*

Case 61
Thomson v Berkhamsted Collegiate School and Others   859

Case 62
Weaver v London Quadrant Housing Trust   875

Case 63
Easyair Ltd (t/a Openair) v Opal Telecom Ltd   882

Case 64
Strydom v Vendside Ltd   886

Case 65
Earles v Barclays Bank plc   906

Case 66
Kris Motor Spares Ltd v Fox Williams LLP   931

Case 67
R v Gray (Richard)   967

Case 68
R v Comer   972

Case 69
R v Ghaffar   980

Case 70
R v Newport   983

Case 71
R v Islami   988

Case 72
R v Phillips   993

Index

Index of Reported Cases (1910–2009)

Table of Cases

Alec Lobb Ltd v Total Oil (GB) Ltd
[1983] 1 WLR 87 .... 901, 903
Armagas Ltd v Mundogas SA (The Ocean Frost)
[1985] 1 Lloyd's Rep 1 913–914
Assicurazioni Generali SpA v Arab Insurance
Group [2003] 1 WLR 577 950
Attorney General of Belize v Belize Telecom Ltd
[2009] UKPC 899

Blomley v Ryan (1954) 99 CLR 362 901
Boycott, Re (1885) 29 Ch D 571 963
British American Tobacco Australia Services
Ltd v Cowell [2002] VSCA 197 916
British Railways Board v Herrington
[1972] 1 AER 786 918

Cave v Robinson Jarvis & Rolf [2003] 1 AC 384 902
Clark v Malpas (1862) 4 De GF & J401 901
Conlon v Simms [2008] 1 WLR 484 955

Dalkia Utilities Services plc v Celtech
International Ltd [2006] EWHC 63 (Comm) 961
Douglas v Hello [2003] EWHC 55 916
Dymocks Franchise Systems (NSW) Pty Ltd
v Todd [2005] 1 Costs LR 52;
[2004] UK PC 39; [2004] 1 WLR 2807 864

Earles v Barclays Bank plc [2009] 6 Costs LR 906 906–930
Easyair Ltd (t/a Openair) v Opal Telecom Ltd
[2009] 6 Costs LR 882 882–885
English v Emery Reimbold & Strick Ltd
[2002] 1 WLR 2409 959

Flannery v Halifax Estate Agents Ltd
[2000] 1 WLR 377 960

Fletcher & Son v Jubb, Booth & Helliwell
[1920] 1 KB 275 927
Floe 884

Godefroy v Dalton (1830) 6 Bing 460 928
Goodson v HM Coroner for Bedfordshire
and Luton [2005] EWCA Civ 1172 .... 877, 878, 879
Grace Shipping v Sharp & Co [1987]
1 Lloyd's Law Rep 207 913–914
Grecoair Inc v John Tilling and Others
[2009] EWHC 115, Queen's Bench 863

Hamilton v Al-Fayed (No. 2)
[2002] 3 Costs LR 389; [2002] EWCA Civ 665 864
Heffer & Knight v Tiffin Green QBENF 97/1050/1 959

India Oil Corporation v Greenstone Shipping SA
[1988] 1 QB 345 919
Infabricks Ltd v Jaytex Ltd [1985] FSR 75 .... 916, 919

Kris Motor Spares Ltd v Fox Williams LLP
[2009] 6 Costs LR 931 931–966

Ladd v Marshall [1954] 1 WLR 1489 956
Laing Management Ltd v Aegon Insurance
Co (UK) Ltd (1997) 86 BLR 961
London Intercontinental Trust Ltd v
Barclays Bank Ltd [1980] 1 Lloyd's Rep 241 926
London Scottish Benefit Society v Chorley
(1883) 16 QBD 872 965
Lord Chancellor v Frieze [2007] 5 Costs LR 684;
[2007] EWHC 1490 (QB) 997, 998

Moorcock, The (1889) 14 PD 64 900
Morris v Wrexham CBC [2001] EWHC Admin 697 876
Multiservice Bookbinding Ltd v Marden [1979] Ch 84 903

Norman, Re (1886) 16 QBD 673 963

Onassis v Vergottis [1968] 2 Lloyds Rep 403 912

PR Records Ltd v Vinyl 2000 Ltd and Others
[2008] 1 Costs LR 19; [2007] EWHC 1721 Chancery 862
R (Corner House Research) v SSTI
[2005] 3 Costs LR 455 ....875, 877, 878
....879, 880
R v Carpenter [41/96] 975
R v Comer [2009] 6 Costs LR 972 ....972, 979
R v Duzgun and Another [2000] 2 Costs LR 316..........983, 986–987
R v Ghaffar [2009] 6 Costs LR 980 980–982
R v Gray (Richard) [2009] 6 Costs LR 967 967–971
R v Islami [2009] 6 Costs LR 988...................................988–992
R v Lord Chancellor, ex parte
Child Poverty Action Group [1999] 1 WLR 347 879
R v Newport [2009] 6 Costs LR 983 983–987
R v Phillips [2009] 6 Costs LR 993.................................993–1000
R v Willard [338/96] 975

Sanders v Isaacs [1971] 1 WLR 240 962
Self v Self [1954] P 480..976
Sheldon v RHM Outhwaite (Underwriting
Agencies) Ltd [1996] AC 102 903
Sibley & Co v Reachbyte Ltd & KMS Ltd
[2009] 2 Costs LR 311; [2008] EWHC 2665 (Ch) 950
Solicitors, In re (1934) Times LR 327......................................962, 963
Strydom v Vendside Ltd [2009] 6 Costs LR 886 886–905

Thomson v Berkhamsted Collegiate School
and Others [2009] 6 Costs LR 859................................859–874

Underwood & Piper v Lewis [1894] QB 306 961

Weaver v London Quadrant Housing Trust
[2009] 6 Costs LR 875 875–881
Williams v Fanshaw Porter & Hazelhurst
[2004] 2 All ER 616 (CA)..904
Winchester Commodities Group Ltd v
RD Black & Co (HC 1999 00894)....................................964
Woods v Martins Bank Ltd [1959] 1 QB 55....................916, 928

Case 61
Thomson

v

Berkhamsted Collegiate School and Others

[2009] 6 Costs LR 859

Neutral Citation Number: [2009] EWHC 2374 (QB)
High Court of Justice, Queen's Bench Division
2 October 2009

Before:
Blake J

Headnote

This case concerned applications for orders to be made ancillary to the hearing of a third party costs claim by the defendant against the Interested Parties who had funded the litigation on behalf of the claimant. The proceedings were discontinued and an order made that the claimant, who was impecunious, pay the defendant's costs. The court considered the jurisdiction to make ancillary orders in costs proceedings, the principles of third party costs awards and the relevance of disclosure and the likelihood of professional privilege arising in respect of the material which was the subject of any disclosure application.

Judgment

Introduction

1. BLAKE J: This is an application for orders to be made ancillary to

the hearing of a third party costs claim made by the defendant school against the non-parties who are hereafter referred to as the interested parties. It is first appropriate to set out the background to the litigation in which the costs application arises.

2. On 16 March 2009, some two weeks into the trial, the claimant, John Thomson, discontinued his claim for damages for injury, loss and damage caused to him through the failure of the defendant, his former school, to take proper measures to prevent him from being bullied. The claimant was born in July 1985. He attended the defendant's school from September 1994 to June 2002. From the autumn term in September 2001 through to the spring of 2002 representations were made on various occasions by John, then aged 17, and his parents, with whom he lived, to teachers and governors at the school complaining of actions by other pupils and the failure of staff to take any sufficient action in respect of it.

3. The proceedings that were discontinued on 16 March 2009 had begun by writ issued on 29 June 2006 and particulars of claim dated 24 October 2006, whereby damages were claimed for negligence alleged between the years of 1996 to 2002.

4. The solicitors acting for the claimant in those proceedings were Linder Myers. They were instructed in February 2005. Before they were involved other solicitors had been instructed by the claimant and/or his parents in connection with concerns as to how the school was treating John. Those solicitors were French and Co. They had communicated with the school in connection with alleged professional negligence or personal injury since April 2002 but it appears their retainer had been terminated by both John and his parents by December 2004. Prior to that termination of retainer there had been an application for pre-action disclosure first intimated in June 2004 and made in November 2004. The application was dismissed and the Master awarded the school its costs of defending the application and payment on account of £1,500 plus VAT was ordered. That sum was paid by Dr and Mrs Thomson, the claimant's parents who are the interested parties in this matter.

5. The litigation in which Linder Myers issued the proceedings was funded as regards the claimant's solicitors, leading and junior counsel, by the interested parties. It seems that consideration had been given to funding by the Legal Services Commission at an earlier stage but no such funding resulted.

6. The defendant school had incurred substantial costs, estimated to have been in excess of £250,000 in defending this action, which they say was wholly misconceived and at the highest would have depended upon facts as to the treatment which the claimant had been subjected which he was unable to prove in his evidence and there was no other material evidence called upon on his behalf to establish that treatment. His father and mother were witnesses on his behalf but on analysis of their evidence it was by and large hearsay evidence, repeating allegations which they say had been made to them by John. By the time the case had been discontinued it was apparent there were substantial problems with respect to any additional evidence that Dr Thomson could give as to John's treatment.

7. The defendant intimated on 16 March 2009 that it was proposing to seek an order for costs against the third parties, pursuant to s 51 Supreme Court Act 1981 and CPR 48.2.

8. On 20 March 2009 the court ordered that the claimant do pay the defendant's costs for the action to be the subject of detailed assessment if not agreed. As the claimant's own case was that he was rendered unemployed and unemployable as a result of the defendant's negligence during his school years there is no reasonable prospect that he will be able to meet these costs from his own resources. On the same date the interested parties were joined as defendants to these proceedings for the purpose only of costs pursuant to CPR 48.2. The court then gave some directions as to pleadings for the grounds of the application and resistance and for the application to be listed before me in due course as the trial judge.

9. Already on that date, counsel for the interested parties appearing through their own solicitors, Irwin Mitchell, contemplated that there may be issues as to disclosure of material documents in the application and the question of legal professional privilege. That issue has loomed large in the written submissions made in support of this application pursuant to the directions given on 20 March 2009 and after.

10. On 30 June 2009 the defendant sought orders of the court requiring Dr and Mrs Thomson to file and serve disclosure statements setting out correspondence between them and Linder Myers and any solicitor previously instructed by either them or the claimant in relation to the subject matter of these proceedings, any correspondence between Dr and Mrs Thomson and any expert or counsel instructed in these proceedings, attendance notes recording meetings, telephone

conversations and other dealings with Dr and Mrs Thomson and any solicitor action in relation to the subject matter of these proceedings. Orders were also sought against the claimant with respect to disclosure and any claim that he may make of legal professional privilege. At that time his solicitors Linder Myers were on the record as representing him and it was anticipated that it would be those solicitors who would prepare the relevant documents and the costs of doing so would be met by the losing party in this application.

11. Skeleton arguments have been served by both counsel for the defendant and the interested parties on the principles which should govern any application for costs pursuant to s 51 and on the sub-issue, the subject of the present application as to whether disclosure should be ordered and how the court should deal with any claim for legal professional privilege that may arise in the course of disclosure.

12. On 21 September 2009 the court heard oral argument on the question and indicated that it would make orders reflecting part of the applications sought by the defendant with reasons to follow. The reasons for that order are given in this judgment.

The Jurisdiction to Make Ancillary Orders in Cost Proceedings

13. The substantive costs application is governed by CPR 48.2 that requires little by way of procedural formality for the determination for such applications other than the service of the funding party as parties to the application. It is reasonably plain from the case law summarised in the notes in the Civil Practice 2009 to this part of the CPR that what is intended is a summary procedure for the determination for such an application.

14. No formal procedure is set out for applications for disclosure, cross-examination, service of skeleton arguments and the like. In my judgment this is because any orders that the court considers necessary are made in accordance with its discretionary judgment in pursuit of its inherent jurisdiction having regard to the over-riding objective and the intended summary nature of the proceedings. However, summary proceedings are not a term of art, and such a description is not inconsistent with whatever other orders the court might consider necessary to expeditiously and fairly determine the substantive issue.

15. Thus it would seem that a hearing of some two days where cross-examination may be ordered is not inconsistent with such proceedings: see *PR Records Ltd* v *Vinyl 2000 Ltd and Others* [2007]

EWHC 1721 Chancery, 18 July 2007 a decision of Mr Justice Morgan at [40]. See also *Grecoair Inc v John Tilling and Others* [2009] EWHC 115, Queen's Bench 14 January 2009 decision of Mr Justice Burton, [42–52]. It is equally plain from those cases that the court has power to exercise disclosure orders in order to facilitate in an economical fashion a fair hearing of the application, although disclosure is often made without formal order.

16. By the end of the hearing in the present matter, the parties were agreed that I had jurisdiction to make the order, but there were competing submissions as to the issues to which I should direct myself in the exercise of my discretion, particularly on the application of the principle of proportionality in the light of the issues in the present case. I am un-persuaded that the appropriate course is to identify the nearest appropriate practice rule applicable to a full trial and add or subtract from the requirements of that rule. I consider that I should apply a high test of what is considered necessary for the fair determination of proceedings that are essentially summary in nature and should be determined speedily after the conclusion of the trial by the trial judge and bearing in mind the over-riding objective. I further recognise that the court's powers are limited where documents are the subject of litigation or legal professional privilege, which it has no power to override. If the court decides that it is necessary and in the interests of justice to make a disclosure order, it may proceed to give a detailed order within its general powers under the CPR to remove outstanding issues that may be the source of delay and further expense if unaddressed. Such an order may include inspection of documents by the court where there is a clear issue as to whether privilege attaches to them.

The Principles on Third Party Costs Awards

17. Before considering whether it is necessary to make the orders the defendant seeks, or any orders, the court needs to consider when a third party costs order is likely to be made in cases of this sort. If the case is weak it is inherently improbable that an order would be made. Alternatively, if it is so overwhelming it seems unlikely that ancillary orders for disclosure, inspection cross-examination or otherwise will be considered really necessary.

18. For present purposes I consider that the law as to third party costs is sufficiently stated at page 1334 of Civil Procedure 2009 and

the judgment of Lord Browne in *Dymocks Franchise Systems (NSW) Pty Ltd v Todd* [2004] UK PC 39; [2004] 1 WLR 2807. I have been assisted by other references to decided cases cited by both counsel in their helpful skeleton arguments on the substantive issues. From this learning I deduce the following general principles of potential relevance to the present case:

i) The order for payment of costs by a non-party would always be exceptional and any application should be treated with considerable caution.
ii) The application should normally be determined by the trial judge who could give effect to any views he had expressed as to the conduct of the non-party without constituting bias or the appearance of bias.
iii) The mere fact that someone has funded proceedings would generally be insufficient to support an application that they pay the costs of the successful party. Pure funders, as described at the case of *Hamilton v Al-Fayed No. 2* [2002] EWCA Civ 665 reported [2003] QB 117 at [40], will not normally have the discretion exercised against them. That definition of "pure funders" means those with no personal interest in the litigation, who do not stand to benefit from it, are not funding it as a matter of business and in no way seek to control its course.
iv) It is relevant but not decisive that the defendant has warned the non-party of the intention to seek costs or that the non-party's funding has caused the defendant to incur the costs it would not otherwise have had to incur;
v) The conduct of the non-party in the course of the litigation and other than as a pure witness of material fact is of relevance and potential weight.
vi) Most of the decided cases on the exercise of the court's discretion under s 51 concerned commercial funders or corporate bodies closely associated with the party who incurred the costs liability which they were unable to satisfy. In the family context, the courts have been reluctant to impose third party costs orders against those family or friends who in the interests of access to justice assist a party to come to court for philanthropic and disinterested reasons.
vii) In determining these applications the court must exercise its case management powers to ensure that the application does not turn

into satellite litigation that results in prolonged, complex and over-extended arguments about costs about costs. For that reason the inherent strength of the application is always a relevant factor.

Relevant Considerations in the Present Application

19. In considering whether, in the light of the particular facts and issues in the case, disclosure is necessary for the fair determination of the application I conclude that I should consider:

i) The strength of the application as it now appears unassisted by disclosure;
ii) The potential value to the fair determination of the application of the documents of which the claimant seeks disclosure and whether they are likely to elucidate considerations highly probative of the exercise of the court's discretion, or threaten to drag the application into a side alley of satellite litigation with diminishing returns for the overall issue;
iii) Whether on a summary assessment it is obvious that the documents for which disclosure is sought will be the subject of proper legal professional privilege;
iv) Whether the likely effect of any order the court might be minded to make will be proportionate and just in all the circumstances.

Strength

20. Although this is a case of family funding I consider that there is strength in the defendant's contention that this is not a case of a pure and disinterested funder who ought not to be at risk of a third party costs order merely because he has made funds available to improve access to justice without seeking to benefit from the proceedings or having an agenda of his own in respect of them. It was plain from the evidence I heard that both Dr Thomson and his wife were very upset from the autumn of 2001 onwards with the school and how it was responding to their letters and requests. It was plain that *they* wanted action to be taken against various children said to have been bullying the claimant, were considering taking independent legal action themselves against them, and threatened the school at an early stage with legal action by themselves. The solicitors instructed between 2002 and 2004 frequently referred to clients plural and included both the claimants and Dr and Mrs Thomson in that description. Elsewhere

there are references to one or other of the interested parties referring to *their* case and *their* claim in correspondence with experts.

21. All in all, there is a quantity of material indicating that the parents were not merely funders but were directly concerned with the facts of the claim, and promoting the remedies that they identified at various points in the history of this matter by way of vindication of their complaints as well as what they perceived to be the damage done to John.

22. Further, there were a number of occasions at the trial when Dr Thomson played a very active role in answering questions in witness statements and elsewhere about the effect of the treatment on John and his earning capacity. I appreciate that the interested parties' case is that their son was a damaged young man who needed much more assistance and support than would normally be the case in a young man of 25 at the date of trial who had successfully completed a degree at Imperial College, London. Nevertheless the fact of intervention in this litigation by the parents beyond the mere question of funding, would be important evidence upon which the defendant could rely in the eventual application to be determined in this case.

23. Particularly important in that context is the defendant's submission about the evidence submitted to the court relating to a diary kept by John and Dr Thomson on his own computer about events that were said to have happened to John in December 2001 and January 2002. There was material supporting the defendant's allegation that Dr Thomson had produced a distorted version of the diary that was made to look like the claimant's own version but included matters different from what the claimant had originally recorded of which Dr Thomson would have had no direct knowledge himself.

24. I also consider that the claim was an unusual one for a number of reasons. These include the chronological extent of the bullying claimed and the school's alleged failure to respond to it. The duration of the pleaded breach of duty was extremely broad going back way before the events of autumn 2001 to a time when John Thompson was a very young boy of nine. In my judgment, taking his evidence at its highest, there was simply nothing that could have properly founded a claim of that nature for such a long period.

25. The real focus of this case was his assertions as to how he was treated by his fellow students in the autumn of 2001 following in

particular the events of the summer of that year after GCSEs had been taken. It was apparent at the hearing that his own conduct towards the girlfriend of a former close friend of his was likely to be the material cause of the termination of that friendship. No physical bullying was alleged by John in his evidence, and on analysis of how he said he was treated from September 2001 onwards, much turned upon his subjective impression of how he was being treated rather than any objective narrative of a course of verbal harassment or oppression of him. This was, at its highest, fragile material on which to found such a serious claim for damages.

26. The damages claim itself was for a very large sum of money by way of lost earnings by reason of the fact that he is said to be unemployable and with virtually no social life. The defendant pointed out that the claimant moved to another school at 17; obtained good A level results and went to a prestigious university, Imperial College, London where he studied for a degree that is notoriously challenging to students and obtained a second class degree that was not a bad result. There were sustained challenges made by the defendant as to the credibility of the evidence of the injury and in particular the real state of his social life.

27. In the light of the evidential difficulties of the claimant's case, I consider there is substance to the suggestion that this litigation was speculative as to its prospects of success. As a result I very much doubt it would have been funded if the interested parties had not made funds available from their own resources. Equally John's parents would be aware of the quantum of costs that were likely to be caused to the defendants by the pursuit of this action, as it does not appear to be substantially different to the funds they made available to their son.

28. This appears to me therefore to be an application for third party costs that has reasonable prospects of success on the merits applying relevant guidance from the decided case law to the court's broad exercise of discretion.

29. However, despite the above, this is an application that does traverse new territory in some respects. This is not a case of a commercial funder or a private or corporate entity that may be regarded as the alter ego of the litigant who was ordered to pay costs. The prospect of John securing a large amount of damages as a result of this litigation would not necessarily directly have benefited the interested parties by putting assets into their own pockets. The hope

for improvement in John's mental state by a successful outcome of this litigation may well be doubted to be an interest of the interested parties' own of a kind comparable to financial benefit.

30. It would, therefore, appear that in so far as either benefit or control was a necessary factor before an order is made (see [18](iii) above), the defendant's best prospects of success would turn upon the extent to which it can point to evidence of control and decision taking in respect of these proceedings.

Relevance of the Disclosure to the Issues in the Application

31. Although the defendant has evidence of the intervention of the interested parties and the extent to which they regarded the cause of legal action against the school their own for the period 2002 to 2004, such material is less prominent for the period after the instruction of Linder Myers in February 2005. Thereafter the *inter partes* correspondence indicates that the claimant's solicitors were careful to always refer to their client as the client alone, in contradistinction of the approach to the previous advisers,

32. It is the costs of the litigation brought by Linder Myers with which I am principally concerned, although it will be for the detailed assessment process to determine if any of the costs incurred before the issue of the Claim Form are properly recoverable. Certainly the costs that might be awarded against the interested parties could be no greater than the costs the claimant is bound to pay.

33. The defendant submits that it can only demonstrate the element of control, interference, and assumption of responsibility in the litigation if it knows what communications the interested parties have had with the solicitors, counsel or expert witnesses in the case. In my judgment, such material, if it exists, is likely to be relevant, and depending on volume, timing, and substance, may well be highly probative of the central disputed issue in the application. It has never been suggested that there was no such correspondence, although the interested parties state that they have no records of written or electronic communications in their possession.

34. However, the case for disclosure is much stronger with respect to the period when Linder Myers were acting for the claimant from February 2005 onwards. I doubt whether the defendants would need details of the correspondence with the earlier solicitors given the evidence that already exists about the parents' interest and relationship

to the issues those representatives were exploring. Restricting the period reduces the scale of the disclosure sought and the practical difficulties that may be encountered in obtaining it if the request were limited to the period, February 2005 to 16 March 2009.

Likelihood of Privilege Existing in Respect of This Material

35. At this point, the court then has to consider whether all such communications are so likely to be the subject of legitimate legal professional privilege as to make the deployment of resources in obtaining discovery futile. The claim to privilege has been made by the claimant personally and not by any solicitor acting for him with knowledge of the material. The solicitors acting for the interested parties are not in possession of the material and not able to make any submissions on whether privilege does in fact apply. The claim seems to be a blanket one in respect of the entirety of the documents sought. There has been no detailed list of documents. No professional lawyer has asserted the existence of privilege after considering the documents and no explanation has been made as to why privilege might exist at all or in respect of all the documents the defendant seeks.

36. Having regard to the general principles as to when legal advice or litigation privilege arises, in my judgment, it would not normally exist in communications between a solicitor and a third party to the claim that were not immediately connected with the witness statement of that third party or the giving of legal advice to the claimant.

37. Communications between the interested parties and any expert witness instructed on behalf of the claimant such as a psychiatrist, psychologist, or educational expert would not normally attract litigation privilege applying general principles.

38. There may be a distinction between the communications between the interested parties and Linder Myers that were done on John's behalf strictly as his agents at a time when he was too distressed or distracted from giving instructions to his solicitors, and more direct communications from the parents themselves. It would seem that only an analysis of the documents could distinguish the two circumstances if a claim was made in that regard.

39. If, as the defendant suspects, there may be material indicating that the interested parties were giving instructions on their own account and without any apparent reference to John's requests, that could be highly probative material in this application which would not

generally be considered to be within the scope of legal professional privilege. Certainly, the interested parties could not claim it as their LPP as they dispute that they were the effective party behind this litigation.

40. I accordingly reach the conclusion that on the information presently available to the court, there may well be material relevant to the determination of this application included within the class identified in revised paragraph one of the court's order herein, that would not be the subject of legal professional privilege and therefore should be the subject of both the disclosure by list and inspection by the defendant thereafter.

Justice and Proportionality

41. I now turn to consider the position of the claimant himself. He is in an odd position. By reason of the court's order of 20 March 2009 he faces a very substantial bill of the defendant's costs that he is wholly unable to meet. He is therefore in peril of bankruptcy that would doubtless further complicate his fragile mental state as revealed in the distress he showed when giving evidence in court, as well as his ability to get on with a career for himself.

42. On 19 March 2009 he signed a form of authority authorising his solicitors at Linder Myers to authorise any client care documents or other documents requested to be disclosed to his parent's solicitors acting in the present proceedings, Irwin Mitchell. It does not appear that Linder Myers disclosed any such documents to Irwin Mitchell pursuant to that authority because the court has had its attention drawn to a letter of 6 April 2009 saying that firm was unaware of the formal authority signed by John and when he discussed the matters with John he only had instructions to disclose a copy of the retainer letter with a CFA with the strict understanding that the documents should be disclosed to Irwin Mitchell alone.

43. The letter stated that the solicitor was not instructed by John to provide such documents. If matters had been disclosed to Irwin Mitchell for the purpose of defending these costs proceedings by John it is difficult to see that any legal professional privilege would prevent them being deployed in these proceedings or being made the subject of disclosure by list. However, if there has been no such disclosure then despite John's apparent willingness to sign a letter of authority on 19 March 2009, he has subsequently changed his mind.

44. The defendant is suspicious that any such change of mind may have been induced by the perception that it may not be in the interests of his parents for this material to come to the court's attention. The defendant understands that John was living at home at this time.

45. In the course of communications between the court and the parties by way of proposed directions and directions for the progressing of this case, the court invited John to waive any legal professional privilege that he may have in any of the documents that the defendant seeks disclosure of in order to reduce costs, in order to expedite the hearing and remove a sub-issue in the application. On 10 August 2009 John wrote a letter addressed to me that was subsequently circulated to the parties as in respect of the request to waive privilege says as follows:

> "I will have to politely decline as I have no idea what that would do to my costs as I do not understand the legal obligations."

It appears that at the time of this letter John had dispensed with the services of Linder Myers who had come off the record in July 2009. That is unfortunate as the defendant's application makes it plain that any costs incurred by John or his solicitors in listing documents that the solicitors must have or have had in their possession of the class corresponding to para 1 of the court's order would be paid for by the successful party in this application, and would not fall on John or Linder Myers. If the defendant's application does not succeed then the only person liable to pay their costs is John himself personally. If John makes a claim to legal professional privilege in respect of the communications by his parents with his solicitors that are not covered by legal professional privilege as the court infers a number of such documents may not be, he will have raised a false issue contributing to further costs in the resolution of this matter.

46. Mr Wignall for the interested parties [suggests] that it would be disproportionate for the court to make the orders requested with the consequences of a difficult problem as to how LPP could be determined and the defendant's application should rest upon strengths or deficiencies of the material as it presently remains. Mr Miller, for the defendant, submits that it is not open to the interested parties to raise the spectre of satellite litigation and disproportionality of the cost of complying, if they do not help themselves by the simple expedient

of requesting from Linder Myers all the documents referred to that they must have readily been able to disclose.

47. It is submitted that there is nothing inconsistent with their obligations to the claimant preventing his solicitors from giving copies of correspondence they have had with the parents. If some of that correspondence did indeed clearly relate to the taking of a witness statement to which litigation privilege would undoubtedly attach it is the solicitors who could most speedily and economically say so. A court would not normally gainsay their expert assessment of the nature of the materials held.

48. Allied to this unwillingness to seek copies of documents of which they were either authors or recipients, the defendant is sceptical of the information that the interested parties have retained none of the documents themselves, whether in a trial bundle format, copy correspondence format, or electronic format on their own computer. Certainly, when he gave evidence, I was impressed with the knowledge of the trial bundles and the detailed procedural history that Dr Thomson demonstrated in his testimony. It was also the case that a number of significant documents had been created by him on his computer, as had letters and representations to various people at various times. It is very surprising that within a short period of time of being on top of this material, the interested parties are telling the court through their solicitors that they have no copy in any form of it. The court has not been informed as to when or how or why they ceased to have access to this material.

49. I am conscious that when John Thomson was last seen in the witness box he frequently broke down in tears and was psychologically fragile, and that was the reason why his treating psychiatrist recommended to his legal team that he discontinued the proceedings. The order that the defendant seeks is that he disclose his documents, as the interested parties claim not to be in possession of their own copies. The court would not seek to impose an onerous obligation on a vulnerable young man, but recognises that there is strength in the defendant's submission that all he needs to do is instruct his solicitors to go through their files and abstract the relevant documents, list them and either permit inspection or make a specific claim to privilege. This should not impose any onerous obligation on John at all. Given that both he and his parents could obtain the documents from Linder Myers there would be a reasonable suspicion

that failure to adopt such a simple course would be evidence of an obstructive intent.

Conclusions

50. In the circumstances I conclude that there is a good arguable case for a third party costs order; that the correspondence sought is likely to be probative and not privileged, at least not in its entirety; and that it is not disproportionate for the material to be sought, at least for the period from February 2005.

51. In my judgment it would be unjust for the defendant to be deprived of the use of such material in pursuit of its application if it proves to be probative and admissible. This is not a fishing expedition, but a pertinent inquiry in the light of the history revealed above.

52. It is in no one's interests to delay the determination of this application for longer than strictly necessary, or to raise false objections, the resolution of which causes further time and expense. My assessment is that with good faith, a method can be found with the co-operation of Linder Myers at the expense of the unsuccessful party in this application that will enable me to know whether there is a credible claim to LPP in respect of a particular document or group of documents falling within the terms of the order. For that to happen the particular documents would need to be individually dated and identified if that is practical or reasonably explained why it is not. Some information must be given as to the subject of the correspondence and the basis of the claim to privilege to see whether it falls into a clear category, no category at all or a debatable category of privilege.

53. The court will then assess the position for itself upon expiry of the time for compliance with these orders and recognises that it may need to inspect documents referred to by either the claimant or the interested parties to ascertain whether LPP exists in respect of a disputable claim. I recognise this means that the court may see documents that it will have to subsequently disregard in its assessment of the issues, if they turn out to be privileged. An economic and efficient way of determining this application permits for no other method. It would not be appropriate to send these documents to another judge to determine since the responsibility for determining this application falls with myself. If a judge is not precluded from determining the application by reason of any strong comments he may

have made during the trial, I do not consider that he would be disqualified by reason of having had to inspect documents to determine the issue of privilege.

54. The court will also be anxious to ensure that this process does not generate opportunities for further disputes and further contested applications before it that would frustrate the object of listing the substantive application in early December for final resolution. Although the court has thus looked ahead to the inspection itself as the necessary means of expeditiously resolving contested issues if they arise, it has not yet decided it will necessarily take that course. Depending upon the material provided in response [to] its orders, the court will reach a judgment on the papers in due course. Parties claiming privilege in documents under their control, will have to be in a position to deliver such documents to the court for its private consideration forthwith if so ordered.

55. By contrast, a failure to comply with these orders, or to adopt simple expedience in good faith to enable the court to have the information that it considers relevant to the fair determination to this application, is likely to lead the court drawing very strong inferences against the party in default.

56. I therefore decided that I should make the orders outlined on September 21 and subsequently perfected. I have reserved the costs of this application to itself and that will receive further consideration in due course.

Andrew Miller (instructed by Berrymans Lace Mawer) appeared for the defendant.

Gordon Wignall (instructed by Irwin Mitchell) appeared for the non-parties joined into the action pursuant to CPR 48.2 for the purposes of costs, Ian and Gracinda Thomson.

Case 62
Weaver

v

London Quadrant Housing Trust

[2009] 6 Costs LR 875

Neutral Citation Number: [2009] EWCA Civ 235
Court of Appeal (Civil Division)
17 February 2009

Before:
Toulson and Elias LJJ

Headnote

This case involved an application for a protective costs order but unusually the application was on behalf of the respondent to an appeal brought by the Trust after it had been given permission to appeal a declaration that it was a public authority by the Divisional Court. The court considered to what extent the guidelines in *R (Corner House Research)* v *SSTI* [2005] 3 Costs LR 455 applied in these circumstances.

Judgment

1. **ELIAS LJ:** This is an application for a protective costs order ("PCO"). The case is due to be heard next week. The applicant is an assured tenant in social housing managed by the defendant trust. The Trust is a registered social landlord under the Housing Act 1996. Apparently it is the seventh largest registered social landlord in the county.

2. The applicant lives with her three children. She was issued with a

notice of possession in March 2007. She sought judicial review before the Divisional Court (Richards LJ and Swift J). At that stage both parties were represented by leading and junior counsel. An important issue for the court was whether the defendant's housing management functions were public functions, with the consequence that the Trust is to be regarded as a "public authority" for the purposes of s 6(3)(b) of the Human Rights Act and is amenable to judicial review. The court concluded that it is a public authority and issued a declaration to that effect. However, the court dismissed the challenge to the notice seeking possession on the facts. The Trust were given leave to appeal the decision insofar as it is reflected in the declaration. They wish to establish that they are not in fact a public authority within the meaning of the Human Rights Act. The matter is considered to be of great concern to registered social landlords throughout the country.

3. The Equality and Human Rights Commission has also sought the right to intervene. They wish to make representations in opposition to the Trust and to support the Divisional Court's decision. So far they have been given the right to make written representations but no right to appear and make oral submissions.

4. It is important to focus on precisely what the applicant is seeking in this application. We have been assisted this morning by Mr Richard Drabble QC. Apparently the position is that the Legal Services Commission will fund this litigation for both junior and leading counsel, but only on condition that they will not be liable for the Trust's costs if the Trust proves to be successful.

5. In my judgment it is important to bear in mind that, when granting leave to appeal, it was certainly open to the court to have made it a condition of the Trust pursuing the appeal not only that they should not undertake not to pursue costs against the claimant, if successful, but in fact that they should bear the costs of both parties in the appeal. The power to impose conditions of that kind is granted by CPR Part 52.37. As an example, in the notes in the White Book the case of *Morris* v *Wrexham CBC* [2001] EWHC Admin 697 is identified as a case where leave to appeal was granted on condition that the appellant pay the respondent's costs of the appeal in any event. Mr Drabble stated that no application was made for a condition of that kind below because it was thought at that stage that the Legal Services Commission would fund the appeal, but in fact they have

taken the position that they will not do so, unless, as I have indicated, the Trust states that it will not pursue its costs if successful.

6. This application is, as I have said, for a protective costs order. The principles which have been developed for providing such orders were set down by the Court of Appeal in the case of *R (Corner House Research) v SSTI* [2005] 1 WLR 2600 at 74. The basic approach is that the court should, in its discretion, do what is fair and just having regard to a number of considerations. The Trust contends that it would be improper to grant the application in the light of these considerations. I will deal with those in a moment.

7. It is, however, worth making a preliminary observation. There can be no doubt that this case is raising an issue of some public importance – of great importance, in particular, to the Trust. It is vital that there is proper representation for both sides before the court. If the claimant does not obtain the PCO that they seek, with the result that they are not represented before the court, then either the Equality and Human Rights Commission would have to take the burden of providing the necessary representation or the court would have to appoint an *amicus*. I have little doubt that if it had been appreciated when leave was granted that the court might have to appoint an *amicus*, permission would not have been granted on that basis. In any event it would now involve a delay to take the step. Perhaps the most important point is that, if either of those two bodies, the *amicus* or the intervenor, were to be running the arguments against the Trust in the appeal, then the Trust would, in any event, not be able to recover any costs against either of them. There is, therefore, a considerable air of unreality about the stance that the Trust is taking, it seems to me. Nonetheless Mr Baker has sought to contend that, if one looks at the relevant criteria set down in the *Corner House* case for determining whether or not a PCO should be granted, then it is plain that it should not be granted in the circumstances of this case.

8. It is a very unusual case, in this regard: although it is plain that a PCO can be granted at any stage in the proceedings and in principle that can even be at the appellate stage (see for example *Goodson v HM Coroner for Bedfordshire and Luton* [2005] EWCA Civ 1172 in the Court of Appeal), nonetheless we have not been referred to any authority which has involved an application for a PCO by somebody who is the respondent to the appeal. The principles appear to have been developed to deal with a case where it is in the public interest that

litigation should be conducted and the litigation would be discontinued if a PCO were not to be made. That plainly is not this case, since the Trust is in control of the appeal and would pursue this appeal whether or not a PCO is granted. It is not possible, it seems to me, to apply the principles set out in the *Corner House* case, particularly at para 74, precisely to the circumstances we have here, but the development of this jurisdiction is a common law development and I am in no doubt that in principle it is appropriate for the applicant to make the application of the kind that has been advanced today.

9. Looking at the considerations which are set out in the *Corner House* case at para 74, Mr Baker does not dispute that some of them are satisfied in this case. Plainly the case raises an issue of general public importance and the public interest requires that the issue should be resolved. Although, in a skeleton argument, he submitted that if one had regard to the financial resources of the applicant and the respondent, it was not necessarily fair and just to make the order because the respondent trust is a charitable body and a non-profit-making body, he has sensibly not pursued that particular submission before us this morning. I have no doubt that the disparity between the financial resources is such that it is not a factor which militates against the making of the order.

10. He does, however, rely upon two features identified by the Court of Appeal in the *Corner House* case, which he says are considerations not met here. The first is that the applicant should have no private interest in the outcome of the case. The significance of that was emphasised in the *Goodson* case, to which I have made reference. That was a case where it was alleged that there had not been a proper investigation into a death, pursuant to Article 2 of the Convention, as there ought to have been. That case failed at first instance, and costs were awarded against the claimant, who then sought a protective costs order for the appeal.

11. One of the issues that was raised before the court was whether it is necessary in all cases that the applicant should have no private interest of any kind in the outcome of the proceedings. It was submitted that it ought not necessarily disqualify the court from making an order that there was some private interest, provided it was outweighed by the public interests involved. Moore-Bick LJ, in his judgment, rejected that submission and concluded that it was a

requirement that there should be no private interest in the outcome of the case. That was consistent with the judgment of Dyson J in *R v Lord Chancellor, ex parte Child Poverty Action Group* [1999] 1 WLR 347, which was a decision which was applied – with some variations – by the Court of Appeal in the *Corner House* case.

12. Mr Baker says that here the applicant has a private interest. She is in a position where, following the declaration from the Divisional Court, she will now have the benefit of public law protection as an assured tenant. I do not accept that that is the kind of private interest which the court was talking about in the *Corner House* case. In the *Goodson* case, to which I have made reference, at para 28 reference was made to the fact that, in some cases, a personal litigant who has standing to apply for judicial review may have a private interest in the outcome of the case in the sense that there will be some benefit, but it is no more than the interest that will apply to the population or a section of the population as a whole. That seems to me to be the position here. This appeal is being conducted in the public interest at the behest of the Trust, not to assert a private interest of the applicant. The possession order against her will stand come what may, and any personal interest she may derive is no greater than that which will accrue to the benefit of all tenants in the same position that she is.

13. The final consideration is whether, if the order were not made, it would result in the applicant discontinuing the proceedings and that it would be reasonable for the applicant to do so. Plainly that consideration cannot apply strictly in those terms in this case. As I have indicated, it is not the applicant who is pursuing the appeal; it is the Trust that is pursuing the appeal. If one applies that consideration by analogy, the question, it seems to me, is whether the effect of refusing the order would be that the applicant would no longer take part in the case and whether she would be acting reasonably in so doing. I have no doubt that it would be reasonable at that stage for her to refuse to take part. She could theoretically be at risk of costs and there is no continuing interest she has in the outcome of the case over and above that which all tenants may have in the outcome. It follows that, in my judgment, if one applies, by analogy, the rules identified in the *Corner House* case to this rather special set of circumstances where the applicant is the respondent to the appeal, then they all are in favour of the PCO being granted.

14. Mr Baker submitted that it was not crucial that the applicant

should be represented, because there is a judgment of the Divisional Court which sets out in some detail the contending arguments. I do not accept that. It is important that this case should be properly argued before the court, and it is not an answer to say that the court could get by with the account of the relevant arguments set out in the judgment of the Divisional Court below.

15. For these various reasons, therefore, in my judgment the criteria for granting the order requested by the applicant are satisfied. The order should be made in terms that the Trust cannot seek to recover its costs against the applicant or against the Legal Services Commission. As I have said, I have absolutely no doubt that that is the condition that could have been imposed when leave was granted. I do not think that the Trust is prejudiced as a result of that order being made at this stage. I am satisfied that the conditions relating to the grant of a PCO are satisfied in the circumstances of this case, particularly given that it is only in those limited terms.

16. **TOULSON LJ:** I agree. I add only a few words because this case does not fall neatly within *Corner House* guidelines. The order of the court below was in an unusual form. It stated:

> "It is ordered that, save for the declaration in para 2 below, the claim is dismissed."

Then followed the declaration about the Trust's amenability to judicial review as a public authority within the meaning of the Human Rights Act 1998, s 6(3)(b). After the court had handed down its written judgment, the Trust sought a formal order in the form just described in order that it should be able to appeal against the declaratory part of the judgment, notwithstanding that the claim for judicial review had itself been dismissed. This was a highly unusual situation. As Elias LJ has observed, it would in those circumstances have been well within the permissible range of the court's powers on considering the application for permission to appeal to have made such permission conditional, at least on the Trust not seeking any order for costs against the respondent or the Legal Services Commission. The Trust might consider itself fortunate that it was not made subject to a condition requiring it to pay both sides' costs of the appeal, since the appeal was being brought in order to establish a point of law of general importance to registered social landlords. It is against that highly unusual background that we come to consider this unusual application. I am satisfied that justice requires it to be granted for the reasons given by Elias LJ.

17. Like him I am puzzled by what the Trust has hoped to achieve by resisting the application. If the application were refused, the respondent would be unrepresented on the appeal. That would be the practical effect, as we understand it. It would be most unsatisfactory that the court hearing the appeal should not be assisted by oral argument on both sides. The only way of achieving that would be either through the intervention of the Equality and Human Rights Commission or by the appointment of an *amicus*. Those are both less obvious methods than by the respondent being represented and if either of those courses were followed the Trust would have no prospect of recovering its costs. In the circumstances I agree that the order should be that the appellant shall not recover any costs in the appeal against either the respondent or the Legal Services Commission.

ORDER: Application granted.

Mr R Drabble QC (instructed by Brian McKenna & Co) appeared on behalf of the applicant.

Mr Baker (instructed by Devonshires) appeared on behalf of the respondent.

Case 63
Easyair Ltd (t/a Openair)

v

Opal Telecom Ltd

[2009] 6 Costs LR 882

Neutral Citation Number: [2009] EWHC 779 (Ch)
High Court of Justice, Chancery Division
8 April 2009

Before:
Lewison J

Headnote

The court considered the appropriate costs order where the substantive issues of breach of contract and fiduciary duty, which had involved the vast majority of evidence and argument and value, were struck out leaving two claims that went to trial and which represented less than 5% of the claims on which the defendant had succeeded. Discussion also took place as to the appropriateness of a costs award on the Indemnity Basis in these circumstances.

Judgment

1. **LEWISON J:** The vast majority of evidence, argument and value concerned the claims for breach of contract and breach of fiduciary duty. Opal was successful in striking out or obtaining summary judgement on those claims. There are two remaining claims that I have allowed to go to trial. Those claims took up little time in preparing evidence or argument and are (on Openair's own assessment) worth less than 5% of the claims on which Opal succeeded. Overall,

therefore, Opal were undoubtedly the successful party. The starting point for any costs order must be that Openair must pay Opal's costs. However, I must also consider whether to make an adjustment in order to reflect the fact that Opal were not completely successful. Two questions arise:

i) Should Opal be deprived of its costs of the issues on which it lost and
ii) If so, should Opal also be ordered to pay Openair's costs of those issues?

2. The issues in question were discrete issues. As Mr Booth points out, the main issue appeared to be whether Openair had received a particular letter. Opal succeeded in demonstrating that it had. The reason why Opal were not successful on the issues that I allowed to go to trial was because of certain points on the construction of the contractual documents which were not the subject of evidence and were barely the subject of argument. It was not unreasonable for Opal to apply for summary judgment on those issues even though they ultimately failed. Moreover, I have not decided those issues in Openair's favour: I have merely decided that they should go to trial. Ultimately Opal may yet succeed on those issues.

3. In all those circumstances I consider that Opal should be deprived of only a small part of its costs; and that I should not require Opal to pay Openair's costs of those issues. I rule, therefore, that Openair must pay 90% of Opal's costs.

4. Opal say that the costs should be assessed on the indemnity basis rather than the usual standard basis. The principal differences between the two measures are:

i) On an assessment on the indemnity basis proportionality has no part to play and
ii) In deciding whether costs were reasonably incurred any doubt is resolved in favour of the receiving party.

5. Mr Booth says that the following features take this case out of the norm and justify an award of costs on the indemnity basis:

i) "Hugely complicated" issues of contract and European law were raised in pursuit of an inflated claim when the basis of that claim was utterly erroneous.

ii) Openair threatened to apply for indemnity costs against Opal in the event that Opal's claim to strike out failed.
iii) Openair accused Opal of improper conduct consisting of illegality and anti-competitive conduct.

6. In my judgment:

i) Although the issues of European law were complicated, the *Floe* decision in the CAT gave some encouragement to Openair. The contractual issues were not complicated at all. That is why I was able to decide them summarily. The fact that a substantial part of a case has failed at the stage of summary judgment does not warrant an award of indemnity costs. The whole point of summary procedures is to stop hopeless cases from going to trial. The giving of summary judgment against a party who has a hopeless case is itself the norm.
ii) Although there is some superficial attraction in the "sauce for the goose" argument, it is only superficial. The fact that one party threatens another with a possible application for indemnity costs does not mean that it is right to accede to that application or to conclude that there is some sort of tacit agreement that costs will be awarded on the indemnity basis.
iii) The accusations of illegality and anti-competitive conduct no doubt increased the heat, but they were not part of the material on which I had to rule.

7. These factors do not in my judgment justify an award of costs on the indemnity basis. Moreover I am concerned about the effect of removing the requirement of proportionality from any assessment of costs. It is true that even on the indemnity basis costs must be reasonably incurred; but the requirement of proportionality is a useful brake on the escalation of costs. I rule, therefore, that Openair must pay 90% of Opal's costs to be assessed on the standard basis if not agreed.

8. It is the usual practice to order an interim payment on account of costs. In the present case Openair has provided security for costs in the shape of an insurance policy. The policy is in the sum of £75,000. Opal estimates its costs in the sum of £109,000-odd. I will order an interim payment of £50,000 to be paid within 21 days.

9. I have also allowed certain amendments to the particulars of

claim. Openair must pay the costs thrown away by those amendments on the standard basis.

10. Openair seek permission to appeal. Ms Anderson has suggested a number of respects in which she says my judgment is open to criticism. However, I would not have given summary judgment if I had concluded that there was doubt about the position. I do not consider that the suggested grounds of appeal have a real prospect of success; and I do not consider that there is any other compelling reason why I should grant permission to appeal. I therefore refuse permission to appeal.

11. What is left of the case should be case managed in Manchester. I will order the case to be transferred to the Manchester District Registry for further directions.

Lesley Anderson QC (instructed by Cobbetts LLP) was for the claimant.

Michael J Booth QC (instructed by Mason Hayes) was for the defendant.

Case 64
Strydom

v

Vendside Ltd

[2009] 6 Costs LR 886

Neutral Citation Number: [2009] EWHC 2130 (QB)
High Court of Justice, Queen's Bench Division
18 August 2009

Before:
Blair J

Headnote

This appeal considered the important principle of whether fees paid to a Claims Handler, which was wholly owned by a Trade Union, during the course of the Vibration White Finger litigation should have been reimbursed to the claimant on the ground that the firm had already negotiated remuneration for its claims handling services with the Government.

Judgment

1. **BLAIR J:** This is an appeal by the claimant, Mr Brian Strydom, from a judgment given by His Honour Judge Inglis in the Nottingham County Court on 6 March 2009 in favour of the defendant, Vendside Ltd, which is a company carrying on business as claim handlers. It is wholly owned by the Union of Democratic Mineworkers (UDM). The judge dismissed Mr Strydom's action to recover a payment he had made to the defendant following the compromise of his claim for an industrial injury called Vibration White Finger (VWF) syndrome (also called Hand-Arm Vibration Syndrome). He says in essence that the

money should be repaid because the defendant was already being compensated for its claim handling services by the Government. In monetary terms, the amount he seeks to recover is very small, £352.50. For that reason, the action was allocated to the fast track. For the same reason, the appeal comes to a single judge of the High Court. However the modest amount at stake belies the fact that the underlying issues are ones of some controversy, and that there are potentially a considerable number of other such claims, which explains the level of legal representation on the appeal and in the court below. There is also the human cost of the illness to the miners concerned. The issues also raise legal questions of some difficulty, and Judge Inglis gave the claimant permission to appeal.

The Judge's Findings of Fact
2. Save in one respect, there is no challenge to the judge's findings of fact. The claimant worked as a miner at Thoresby Colliery in Nottinghamshire between 1982 and 1993. He remained a member of the UDM until 1997, and during the course of his membership, the union pursued various claims for personal injury on his behalf. His claim in respect of VWF syndrome arose as follows. In 1998, the High Court approved a Scheme for the compensation of coal miners and former miners who as a result of their work suffered from this disease. By then, the Government had taken on the personal injury liabilities of the British Coal Corporation, which had been the claimant's employer. There were many potential claims outstanding. Mr Robert Glancy QC for the claimant told me that there were about 170,000 in relation to VWF amounting some £1.6 billion. When one adds to that the approximately 580,000 potential claimants in respect of chronic obstructive pulmonary disease incurred by people working in the mines, which was subject to its own Scheme set up at the same time, one can see that the amounts involved were very large indeed.

3. So as to deal with these claims (the vast majority of which were likely to be undisputed) the Government appointed its own claims handlers, a company called IRISC Claims Management, to handle the Scheme. The Government through the Department of Trade & Industry (DTI) also entered into claims handling agreements with service providers on the claimants' side so that the interest of individual miners could be represented. One such claims handling agreement (CHA) was with the defendant company. It is dated 29

January 1999. It provides for a single claims handling fee in respect of VWF syndrome to be paid. This was originally in the sum of £550 plus VAT and from the end of January 2000 in the sum of £500 plus VAT. The fee was increased at a later date to £600 plus VAT. In addition, the defendant was entitled to receive "reasonably incurred/previously agreed disbursements".

4. Under the CHA, the defendant was responsible for the submission of a letter of claim with details that were derived substantially from the questionnaire filled in by the claimant in question. It also had to consider whether such claimant was within the compensation Scheme at all. A medical report would then be prepared and paid for by the DTI, and usually, when the Scheme became established, arranged by it. Settlement would then be negotiated between the defendant and IRISC. Cases that could not be settled came out of the Scheme and thereafter would be subject to normal litigation. The Scheme contained clear parameters for both liability and quantum.

5. In 1998, the claimant heard of the Scheme, and he got in touch with the union and was referred to the defendant. On 23 September 1998, he submitted a completed questionnaire and entered into a written agreement. This was a standard form agreement that the defendant used for this and many thousands of such claims put through the Scheme in subsequent years. Though it predated the CFA by a few months, the defendant accepted that it handled VWF claims prior to the date of the CFA pursuant to the terms contained in that agreement or terms substantially to the same effect.

6. The agreement consisted of a form dated 23 September 1998 and headed "VIBRATION WHITE FINGER" on the notepaper of the Union of Democratic Mineworkers, Nottingham Section. The claimant had to fill it in, and sign it. There were two options to choose from as follows:

> "1* Agree that if my Claim is *successful* I will pay to Vendside Ltd, who administer these Claims, a fee, to cover the cost of pursuing this Claim on my behalf, within the following guidelines:
>
> *Settlement Amount Fee Payable*
>
> | | |
> |---|---|
> | Up to £500.00 | £50.00 + VAT |
> | £500.01 – £1000.00 | £100.00 + VAT |
> | £1000.01 – £1500.00 | £150.00 + VAT |

etc. in increments of £50 + VAT for every £500 recovered, up to a maximum of £300 + VAT on a settlement of £3,000 or more.

Cheques should be made payable to: 'VENDSIDE LTD' and will be required at settlement of the Claim

2* I confirm that I am at present a Full Financial member of the UDM Nottingham Section and, therefore, No 1 above does not apply to me. I also confirm that in the event of my leaving the Industry I agree to pay an equivalent sum to the current Union contribution until my Claim is finalised."

7. As the terms of the form make clear, had the claimant been a paid up member (a "Full Financial member") of the union, he would have opted for the second choice, and there would have been no fee payable in the event of a successful claim. However, he was not by then a paid up member, and so he opted for the first choice. The effect of the agreement was that if his claim was successful, he would pay a fee to "cover the costs of pursuing this Claim on my behalf" on a sliding scale depending on the settlement amount. In due course, his claim was processed. He was advised to, and did, reject at least one offer that was thought to be insufficient. In June 2000, he accepted an improved offer of £10,545.

8. By a letter dated 15 June 2000, he authorised the defendant to accept this sum in settlement of his claim. On the sliding scale, since this settlement exceeded £3000, the maximum amount of £300 plus VAT mentioned in the letter of 23 September 1998 was payable. The letter goes on to state that, "I also understand that as a non-financial member of the UDM I agree to pay £300.00 plus VAT to cover the cost of pursuing this claim on my behalf, as such I attach a cheque to the value of £352.50 in payment of same". In due course, the claimant received his compensation.

9. The present action comes to be brought in the following circumstances. In 2004, Mrs Strydom contacted Mr John Mann who is MP for Bassetlaw about the £352.50 which had been paid by her husband. Mr Mann took the cause up on behalf of miners who had brought claims for compensation but who had paid a fee to handlers such as the defendant, or to firms of solicitors, or others. The controversy that followed was that the claims handlers had already been paid a full and proper fee by the DTI but had taken an additional

fee from claimants. Mr Mann elicited various Parliamentary answers from the Minister. On 3 February 2004, the Minister said that "with regard to the work of claim handling agents we have included in all our publicity material ... reference to the fact that there should be no need for any organisations processing claims to charge claimants a fee or deduct any compensation and if any claim handling firms suggest other arrangements claimants should seek advice elsewhere". On 21 June 2004, the Minister answered that, "I am advised that at no time has the department agreed that third parties can charge additional sums". By that time, of course, Mr Strydom had long ago paid his fee. These proceedings were begun by him on 28 January 2005. A large number of similar claims were then intimated or brought. This claim and others were stayed whilst an application was made to the High Court for a Group Litigation Order. That application (in the judge's words) proved misguided, and was firmly dismissed by Sir Michael Turner on 18 May 2006 (who as a High Court judge had approved the original Scheme). The present action was then restored, and is apparently the first one to come to a hearing.

10. Against that background, the judge made a number of specific findings of fact some of which may be material as regards the appeal. The origin of the practice by which people who were paying their membership contributions to the union were dealt with differently from people who were not paying them was as follows. In the 1990s, the UDM's claims handling operation had expanded considerably leading ultimately to the establishment of the defendant company. In processing claims, the union would incur expense, particularly in respect of disbursements, and ran the risk of being out of pocket in respect of unsuccessful claims. Union members who had paid their subscriptions up to date received representation free. Members who had retired or others who had never been members would have been favoured unfairly if they had the benefit of the union's representation but did not have to make any financial contribution. The fee charged to such persons was "in lieu of membership" and pitched a level approximate to two years membership of the union, or £300, two years being the kind of period that it might be expected to take to pursue a claim.

11. That system was carried over into representation under the CHA schemes. As the judge pointed out, the difference in this instance was that the DTI paid a fee for each claim that was successful. The

Scheme overall, even taking into account the fact that the defendant received no payment for unsuccessful cases, was very profitable. The profitability of the business could be seen by the effect on the defendant company's shareholder funds (represented in the accounts by net cash). The judge said that they rose from a modest deficit in 1998 to a credit of over £8m by the end of 2006.

12. The judge went on to consider the question whether the flat rate fee paid by the DTI in respect of successful cases was sufficient remuneration for work overall. The clear answer, he held, is that it was. He heard evidence from Mr Michael Stevens, who since 1993 has been General Secretary of the UDM. Mr Stevens told him that at the outset, it was not clear that the DTI was going to pay enough, or that the volume and nature of the claims would be such as to make handling the claims for the fee paid by the DTI viable. The judge did not accept that evidence. He found that it was understood from the outset that the fee was going to be such that handlers receiving it were not going to make a loss from their involvement in the Scheme. The fee was pitched at such a level as to amount to adequate remuneration.

13. The CHA did not preclude in its terms the defendant from charging a further fee to claimants. Mr Stevens maintained that the DTI knew that the trade unions were going to charge a fee to individual successful claimants. In this regard, the judge held that it was not necessary to resolve the question who knew what, having found that the fee was pitched at such an amount that was expected to make participation in the scheme viable and indeed profitable from the defendant's point of view. The judge did however say that, "It appears to me unlikely that it was contemplated by those who negotiated the fee payable to claims handlers that any claims handler would effectively be taking a slice of the compensation as well. If that were to have been regarded as legitimate it would necessarily have affected the amount of the fee agreed and would have been the subject of negotiation. It suffices in my judgment to find as I do that the level of the fee arrived at was such an amount as to be, and to be understood as being, adequate remuneration for the claims handlers' work."

14. In his first statement of 23 September 2005, the claimant had said that he was a fully paid up member of the union, and so did not understand why he was charged a fee. As the judge pointed out, the claimant was wrong in his recollection in that respect. In a subsequent statement of 6 December 2008, he said that it was not made clear or

explained to him that he had the freedom to approach a solicitor as an alternative to using the defendant. If he had understood this to be the case he would have sought help from an appropriate firm of solicitors without the need to incur a claims handling fee. The claimant unfortunately is seriously ill, and was unable to attend trial to give evidence. The defendant submitted that in the absence of evidence that could be tested in cross examination, there was no credible evidence upon which the court could find in the claimant's favour in this respect. However the judge said that there was nothing about the claimant's state of knowledge in the defendants' witness statements:

> "It could not seriously be suggested that the claimant knew of the funding arrangements between [the defendant] and the DTI where the [defendant itself] avoided telling him anything about them, and where there is no evidence to undermine what he says, namely that he found out the facts in 2004. His absence from the witness box is unfortunate but there is no reason at all to think that his account on that crucial issue would be undermined."

15. Another factual question at trial was what would have happened had the claimant been told that the defendant was being paid a handling fee by the DTI and that a contribution from him was not in fact necessary to cover the cost of pursuing the claim on his behalf. If the full facts had been known to the claimant in 1998, the judge found that the fee would not have been levied from him, but that if the defendant had insisted upon it, on balance the claimant (and no doubt very many other miners) would have gone elsewhere. On the other hand, he did not find that the defendant knew that others would or might provide the service that it was providing without any charges to the claimant concerned. The defendant's officers "may or may not have known that but the evidence does not satisfy me that they did know that some solicitors for example charged a fee and some did not".

16. There is one further factual matter which arises strictly speaking in relation to limitation only, though the claimant has relied upon it in relation to liability generally. It was held that in contracting to receive the £352.50, the defendant (through Mr Stevens and Ms Walker) deliberately did not disclose that it was to receive payment for its work from another source to cover the cost of pursuing the case: "In my judgment they knew, since it was obvious, that had they revealed the

fact people in the position of Mr Strydom would have questioned it." In making that finding, the judge rejected the defendant's submission that the claimant's evidence from the witness box and testing of it in cross examination would be necessary. The defendant submits that the evidence did not justify this conclusion, and in this regard only the judge's findings of fact are challenged on the appeal. I shall deal with this challenge when considering limitation. It is right to express appreciation for the thoroughness of the judge's findings, reached after a trial that lasted a day only, during which there was a considerable body of evidence and legal submission.

The Claimant's Pleaded Case

17. In broad terms, the claimant's case is that whilst arrangements of the kind set out in the agreement letter of 23 September 1998 may have been justified under earlier conditions prevailing in the union, they were objectionable in the present case because the defendant was going to get paid by the Government for the service it provided under the terms of the CHA. The claimant contends that he is entitled in law to recover the sum he paid on three bases: the first is in reliance on a term said to be implied into the contract, the second is in reliance on a concurrent duty in tort (though that has not been pursued in argument), and the third asserts that the bargain entered into by the parties was unconscionable.

18. The relevant paragraphs of the amended particulars of claim (leaving out amendments) are as follows.

"14.

(1) It was an implied term of the said agreement between the claimant and the defendant that the defendant owed the claimant duties of care as if the defendant was acting as a solicitor retained by the claimant, including the duty to act with reasonable care and skill, the duty to give fair, full frank and honest advice to the claimant, the duty to advise the claimant of any actual or potential conflict of interest between the claimant, the defendant and UDM and the duty not to misrepresent by statement or omission, the claimant's liability for the cost of pursuing the said claim or the defendant's entitlement to costs under and pursuant to the said arrangement.

(2) The defendant owed the claimant concurrent duties to those set out in para 2 hereinabove in tort; ...

16. In the premises the claimant will contend that:
(i) By failing to disclose the fact referred to in para 14 herein above and/or
(ii) Requiring the claimant to sign the said agreement and/or to pay the said sum of £352.50 in the belief that he had to do so in order to have his claim handled by and/or to remunerate the defendant for the cost of pursuing the said claim and/or
(iii) In failing to advise the claimant that he could pursue the said claim through a solicitor at no cost whatsoever to himself.

The defendant:
(i) Was in breach of the said implied terms of the said agreement and was negligent;
(ii) Caused or permitted the claimant to enter into an unconscionable bargain."

19. The defendant made certain admissions as to what was implied into the contract but otherwise denied the claim. The claimant places considerable reliance upon these admissions. The relevant paragraph of the Amended Defence is as follows.

"17. In relation to para 14(1) of the amended particulars of claim:
a. It is admitted that it was an implied term of the contract between the claimant and the defendant that the defendant would, in handling the claimant's VWF claim, act with reasonable skill and care and give fair, full, frank and honest advice to the claimant in relation to the merits of his claim and its handling thereof;
b. It is specifically denied that it was an implied term of the contract between the claimant and the defendant that the defendant would owe to the claimant the same duties as if the defendant was acting as a solicitor retained by the claimant, which it manifestly was not;
c. It is denied that it was an implied term of the contract between the claimant and the defendant that the defendant would advise the claimant of any actual or potential conflict of interest whether as alleged or at all;
d. It is denied that it was an implied term of the contract between the claimant and the defendant that the defendant owed to the claimant

any duty not to misrepresent by statement or omission, the claimant's liability for the costs of pursuing his said claim or the defendant's entitlement to costs under and pursuant to its agreement with the DTI."

In para 24, it is denied that the contract between the claimant and the defendant was an unconscionable bargain.

The Parties' Cases on Appeal

20. It is evident from the amendments to the particulars of claim that a number of the ways in which the claimant originally sought to put his case have not subsequently been pursued. It is no longer contended that a fiduciary relationship existed between the parties (a point on which the defendant placed some emphasis during argument). A claim under the Unfair Terms in Consumer Contracts Regulations 1999 is not pursued, nor a claim in undue influence. Also deleted by amendment is a claim that the defendant falsely and negligently represented to the claimant that he was obliged to pay the sums in question. In the course of oral argument on the appeal, Mr Glancy QC also made it clear that he was no longer arguing that the duty owed by the defendant was the same as that of a solicitor. By the same token, no claim by reference to conflict of interest is pursued. It is no longer alleged that the contract can be impugned on the basis that there was no or no adequate consideration. It is understandable that the claim should have been widely pleaded, because by the time it came to be brought, there were incipient limitation difficulties. In the light of the evidence, the case has been whittled down to what is seen as properly arguable.

21. I begin with the claimant's case as to implied term. The judge began by observing that the case was not put on the basis that there was a misrepresentation that induced the contract. That is right, as was made clear by Mr Glancy at trial and on the appeal. The judge referred to the:

"difficulty of implying a term of the kind contended for by the claimant which goes far beyond what is necessary for the working of this simple contract. Nor is it possible to read into the terms of that simple contract an obligation on Mr Strydom to pay the sum stipulated only in the event that it was necessary to pay it to compensate the defendants for the work that they did. The defendants undertook to perform work which if it resulted in success would involve the claimant in payment of a specific sum of money. Nothing could be simpler. I do not think that there is any basis for implying a term requiring disclosure as part of the contractual or other duties of the defendants, non compliance of which would result in breach of contract or breach of common law duty. What is contended for is quite different from the admitted term of reasonable care and skill in carrying out the contract which is obviously necessary to establish a duty to do the work contracted for adequately."

22. Mr Glancy has submitted that in making these observations, the judge failed to appreciate that the claimant's case was that the defendant was under an implied duty not to misrepresent by statement or omission the claimant's liability for the cost of pursuing the claim. It was wrong he says to regard this as a "simple contract", and in any case the judge wrongly treated it as a commercial arrangement, whereas the circumstances were unusual if not unique. In those circumstances, the defendant was under a duty not to misrepresent the situation to the claimant nor to mislead him explicitly or implicitly into thinking that he had to pay the fee to cover the cost of pursuing the claim on his behalf. The judge's reference to the admitted term of reasonable care and skill showed (Mr Glancy submitted) a "comprehensive failure to appreciate the claimant's argument on this point", because the defendant's admission went substantially further admitting an implied term that the defendant would "give fair, full, frank and honest advice to the claimant in relation to ... its handling [of his claim]". It is said that if the judge had approached the issue on the basis of the implied term as admitted by the defendant, he would have had to find that the advice given to the claimant was not fair, full, frank or honest. The claimant also submits that his conclusions on this point are inconsistent with his finding of deliberate concealment in relation to limitation.

23. Mr James Allen QC for the defendant submits that the question was whether the implied term pleaded by the claimant was necessary to give business efficacy to the contract, and the judge correctly held that it was not. So far as the admission as regards advice is concerned, it is argued that such duty can have come into existence only after the contract itself came into existence. It cannot therefore have been any part of the duty to advise the claimant that he would have to pay £300 to the defendant in the event of his claim being successful, since by the

time any such duty came into existence, the claimant was already contractually bound to make the payment. It is said that the claimant's case relies upon the fallacious contention that a contract may contain an implied term which imposes retrospective duties upon one of the parties. In any case, it is submitted that no advice was given, rather that the defendant informed the claimant that if he wished the defendant to handle his case he would have to pay it that sum.

24. As regards the case as to unconscionable bargain, the judge said that the court could only intervene if the defendant's behaviour was unconscionable, and the outcome was oppressive to the claimant. He considered that there was nothing in the case which would entitle the court to give relief outside the parameters of misrepresentation and breach of contract. The claimant argues that he was wrong not to find that the bargain struck between the claimant and the defendant was unconscionable because the defendant's conduct in extracting from him a promise to pay £352.50 if his claim was successful to cover the costs of pursuing the claim was improper, unfair and exploited the claimant's lack of knowledge and understanding in a morally culpable manner, and in a way which should shock the conscience of the court. The judge should have ordered the rescission of the bargain, and the return of the contractual sum plus interest. The defendant on this point submits that the judge decided the issue correctly for the reasons that he gave.

Discussion

25. The large amounts of money amounts paid to advisers in connection with miners' compensation claims have been a matter of public concern, but Mr Glancy QC did not suggest that this was relevant to the outcome of the appeal. Whatever the underlying considerations may be, to succeed on the appeal, the claimant has to show that his claim is soundly based in law. In essence, the claimant says that it is unfair that he should have to pay for the defendant's claims handling service when the DTI was already paying for it, a fact that was not disclosed to him at the time he entered into the contract, or indeed afterwards. This is not, he points out, a commercial context, but rather one in which a former miner was looking to his union for help. He argues that in these circumstances, the court should find a way to allow the claim, by implying a term that enables recovery of the

amount he paid, or alternatively by setting the contract aside as an unconscionable bargain.

26. The defendant on the other hand points out that the service it provided to the claimant would have been provided for nothing had his union dues remained up to date. The reason for making a charge for people like him was so as to treat equally those who were paying their dues, and those who were not, but who nonetheless wanted to use the services of the union to handle a claim on their behalf. Mr Strydom got what he bargained for. The union successfully pursued his claim, and it would be unfair to allow him to recover back the fee which he agreed to pay in such circumstances.

27. Since this is an appeal, the claimant must bring himself within CPR Part 52.11(3), by which the appeal court will allow an appeal where the decision of the lower court was wrong. I have approached this question in accordance with the commentary contained at para 52.11.4 of the White Book.

Implied Term

28. The case is put on the basis of a term said to be implied into the contract between the parties. The implied term which is pleaded is that the "Defendant owed the claimant duties of care as if the defendant was acting as a solicitor retained by the claimant, including the duty to act with reasonable care and skill, the duty to give fair, full frank and honest advice to the claimant, the duty to advise the claimant of any actual or potential conflict of interest between the claimant, the defendant and UDM and the duty not to misrepresent by statement or omission, the claimant's liability for the cost of pursuing the said claim or the defendant's entitlement to costs under and pursuant to the said arrangement". As mentioned, the term contended for has been cut down, in that it is not argued on appeal that the union's duty was the same as that of a solicitor or included a duty to advise as to conflict of interest. Mr Glancy made it clear in his submissions in reply that he was not contending for a duty of disclosure – the case was put on the basis that there was a duty not to mislead as regards costs. His argument was put in two ways, the first being based on admissions in the defence, and the second being based on the ordinary principles by which a court will imply terms into a contract.

29. It was admitted in the defence that "it was an implied term of the contract between the claimant and the defendant that the

defendant would, in handling the claimant's VWF claim, act with reasonable skill and care and give fair, full, frank and honest advice to the claimant in relation to the merits of his claim and its handling thereof". Mr Glancy argues that the judge failed to appreciate that his argument in this respect was not concerned with the "reasonable skill and care" part of this admission, but with that part of the pleading by which the defendant admitted that it was under a duty to give advice to the claimant in relation to the handling of his claim.

30. In substance, this part of the argument turned on the scope of the defendant's admission. It appears to me that the duty contended for is not within the admitted term as to the giving of advice as to the merits of the claim and its handling. A "duty not to mislead" is given effect to (if it arises) by a claim in misrepresentation, which is not pursued in this case. Further, I do not think that the judge overlooked the scope of the admission. It is correct, as Mr Glancy points out, that in para 24 of the judgment, the judge states the admission by reference to reasonable care and skill, without referring expressly to the second part of the admission dealing with advice. But he set out the full admission as it appeared in the Amended Defence earlier in his judgment. He also set out the later passage in the Amended Defence which denied that it was an implied term of the contract that the defendant owed to the claimant any duty not to misrepresent by statement or omission the claimant's liability for the costs of pursuing his claim or the defendant's entitlement to costs under and pursuant to the CHA, the term the claimant is arguing for. Thus the judge was aware that the defendant was denying the claimant's case in this respect, and I do not consider that it was within the admission.

31. The second way the argument is put is that the term contended for is to be implied into the contract on ordinary principles. Mr Glancy refined the pleaded term slightly in oral argument, arguing for a "continuing" duty not to misrepresent by statement or omission the claimant's liability for the costs of pursuing his claim or the defendant's entitlement to costs under and pursuant to the CHA. (This was intended to deal with the defendant's submission that a term cannot be implied into a contract which imposes retrospective duties upon one of the parties.) There were no detailed submissions by either party of the appropriate test for implication of terms (cf. the recent decision of the Privy Council in *Attorney General of Belize* v *Belize Telecom Ltd* [2009] UKPC). The appeal proceeded on the basis that

the test for implying a term is necessity, reliance being placed on *The Moorcock* (1889) 14 PD 64, and in particular the classic statement of Bowen LJ at 68:

> "In business transactions such as this, what the law desires to effect by the implication is to give such business efficacy to the transaction as must have been intended at all events by both parties who are business men."

32. That case establishes that a term is to be implied into a contract because it is necessary, in the business sense, to give efficacy to the contract. Having accepted that this is the correct test in law, Mr Glancy submitted however that the present situation was a unique one, and that the approach that would be taken to a commercial contract should not be applied here. He says that it is necessary to imply the term into this contract because "otherwise one has the situation where the defendant company is enabled to earn enormous sums from the public, and at the same time to charge retired miners what for them is a significant sum, and one which the Government is already paying".

33. It is certainly true that each contract is different, and that this contract was not the type of complex commercial arrangement that features in some of the case law. It is also true that the background has some features which are probably unique. But that does not mean that the question of implication is in the court's discretion, or that the court has power to introduce terms to make the contract fairer or more reasonable. As noted, the claimant does not suggest that he is entitled to rescind the contract on the basis of a misrepresentation as to fees. Nor does he rely on a freestanding duty of disclosure. Nor is it suggested that the relationship between the parties was a fiduciary one. The question the judge was asked to decide was whether the asserted term was necessary to give it efficacy. He took the view, correctly in my opinion, that it went far beyond what was necessary in what was, in essence, a simple contractual arrangement. Putting the question in a different way, I do not consider that the letter of 23 September 1998, read as a whole against the relevant background, would reasonably be understood to include the term contended for. The legal threshold for the implication of terms is not satisfied, and in my view, the judge was right so to hold. Mr Glancy did not suggest in either written or oral argument that a different result would follow in tort, and I need say nothing more about the position in tort.

Unconscionable Bargain

34. As regards unconscionable bargains, the claimant submits that on the judge's findings of fact, there has been impropriety and unfairness in the bargaining process and that such impropriety is to be found in the conduct of the stronger party. The fact that this case is different from earlier authority, it is submitted, does not mean that equity cannot intervene. Equity will intervene in any case where there has been unconscionable behaviour. The defendant for its part submits that the judge rightly held that the contract was not an unconscionable bargain as that term is understood in the law.

35. The judge directed himself on this issue by applying the well known dictum of Mr Peter Millett QC (as then was) in *Alec Lobb Ltd v Total Oil (GB) Ltd* [1983] 1 WLR 87 (reversed in part at [1985] 1 WLR 173). On the basis of the case law, it was held at pages 94–95 that three elements must be present before the court will interfere with a contract on this basis:

> "First, one party has been at a serious disadvantage to the other, whether through poverty, or ignorance, or lack of advice, or otherwise, so that circumstances existed of which unfair advantage could be taken: see, for example, *Blomley v Ryan* (1954) 99 CLR 362, where, to the knowledge of one party, the other was by reason of his intoxication in no condition to negotiate intelligently; secondly, this weakness of the one party has been exploited by the other in some morally culpable manner: see, for example, *Clark v Malpas* (1862) 4 De GF & J401, where a poor and illiterate man was induced to enter into a transaction of an unusual nature, without proper independent advice, and in great haste; and thirdly, the resulting transaction has been, not merely hard or improvident, but overreaching and oppressive. Where there has been a sale at an undervalue, the under-value has almost always been substantial, so that it calls for an explanation, and is in itself indicative of the presence of some fraud, undue influence, or other such feature. In short, there must, in my judgment, be some impropriety, both in the conduct of the stronger party and in the terms of the transaction itself (though the former may often be inferred from the latter in the absence of an innocent explanation) which in the traditional phrase 'shocks the conscience of the court', and makes it against equity and good conscience of the stronger party to retain the benefit of a transaction he has unfairly obtained."

36. In summary, therefore, before the court will consider setting a contract aside as an unconscionable bargain, one party has to have been disadvantaged in some relevant way as regards the other party, that other party must have exploited that disadvantage in some morally culpable manner, and the resulting transaction must be overreaching and oppressive. No single one of these factors is sufficient – all three elements must be proved, otherwise the enforceability of contracts is undermined (see the reasoning in Goff & Jones, *The Law of Restitution*, 7th edn, para 12-006). Where all these requirements are met, the burden then passes to the other party to satisfy the court that the transaction was fair, just and reasonable (*Snell's Equity*, 31st edn, para 8-47).

37. As to the first requirement, the judge accepted that there was inequality of bargaining power between a former miner looking for advice and trusting the union to look out for his interests, and the union offering to pursue the miner's claim on its own terms and for its own benefit. (I think that this must be treated as a finding on the particular facts, because the concept of "inequality of bargaining power" will normally have no place in the relationship between a union and its members.) But, he held, it was essential that the outcome was oppressive to the claimant, and that in addition the defendant must have acted unconscionably. As to unconscionable behaviour, he said:

> "Neither the consequences of the contract nor the conduct of the defendant's, even if regarded as reprehensible, qualifies for that sort of relief. To turn failure to disclose into conduct which will allow the court to intervene in equity in my judgment is to take the powers of the court too far ..."

The claimant has submitted that this passage shows that the judge found that the defendant's conduct was reprehensible. In my view however the defendant is correct to submit that it is implicit from this passage of his judgment that he did not make such a finding.

38. To support his argument, Mr Glancy QC referred to *Cave v Robinson Jarvis & Rolf* [2003] 1 AC 384. This was a case about deliberate concealment for the purposes of s 32(1)(b) Limitation Act 1980. It had been submitted that some degree of unconscionability in the conduct of the defendant is necessary before this provision can deprive a defendant of a limitation defence. At [64], Lord Scott said

that, "This was, I think, based mainly on Lord Browne-Wilkinson's comment in *Sheldon v RHM Outhwaite (Underwriting Agencies) Ltd* [1996] AC 102, 145h that 'unconscionable behaviour by deliberately concealing the facts relevant to the plaintiffs' cause of action' was 'the underlying rationale' of s 32". Lord Scott continued at [65], "I respectfully agree that it is difficult to think of a case of deliberate concealment for s 32(1)(b) purposes that would not involve unconscionable behaviour". Mr Glancy has sought to invoke this passage to show that the judge's finding that this case falls within s 32(1)(b) Limitation Act 1980 necessarily involved a finding that there has been unconscionable behaviour by the defendant in this case. But the argument loses force when one appreciates that Lord Scott went on to hold that the "statutory language does not require that the behaviour of the defendant is unconscionable and its addition as a criterion to be satisfied before a case can be brought within s 32 is, in my opinion, unnecessary and unjustified". In the event, Judge Inglis did not make such a finding.

39. Furthermore, I think that he was right so far as he held that the third element identified in *Lobb*, namely that the transaction was oppressive, was not shown on the facts of this case. As *Chitty on Contracts*, 30th edn, at paras 7-129 and 7-130 makes clear, before it will be treated as an unconscionable bargain, a contract must be oppressive to the complainant in its overall terms. The question is whether the contract was oppressive, not whether it was unreasonable – this appears, for example, from *Multiservice Bookbinding Ltd v Marden* [1979] Ch 84 in which Browne-Wilkinson J said at p. 110, "it is not enough to show that, in the eyes of the court, [the bargain] was unreasonable". The question must, I think, be determined on the facts as they are at the time the contract is entered into, and from the perspective of the disadvantaged contracting party. Whilst I have considerable sympathy with the claimant's submissions, persuasively put by Mr Glancy QC, the fact is that he had to pay a fee because he was seeking union representation and was no longer paying his union dues, the fee was payable only in the event of a successful settlement, and it was capped at £300. It is correct that the union was also to receive a fee from the DTI, and that this activity turned out to be very profitable given the number of claims that were handled. But legitimate public concern on this ground does not render the contract "oppressive" in the legal sense as regards the claimant. The issue

whether or not the DTI might have had a cause of action does not arise in this litigation. Applying the above principles, I consider that the appeal on this point also fails.

Limitation

40. In view of my findings on the claimant's appeal, it is not strictly necessary to deal with the limitation issue, which was decided in favour of the claimant. By a respondent's notice, the defendant asserts that there was no evidence upon which to find that the defendant deliberately did not disclose that it was to receive payments from another source. On that basis, it is submitted that the judge was wrong to hold, as he did, that the claim in contract was not time barred by virtue of s 31(1)(b) Limitation Act 1980. This section provides that where any fact relevant to the plaintiff's right of action has been deliberately concealed from him by the defendant, the period of limitation shall not begin to run until the plaintiff has discovered the concealment, or could with reasonable diligence have discovered it. So, it is submitted, the judge was wrong to decide that time did not begin to run until 2004 when (as he held) the claimant found out about the DTI payments.

41. The defendant cites the discussion in *Williams v Fanshaw Porter & Hazelhurst* [2004] 2 All ER 616 (CA) at [14] of the requirement that the fact relevant to the right of action must be "deliberately concealed". In that passage, Park J said that "for concealment to be deliberate, the defendant must have considered whether to inform the claimant of the fact and decided not to. I would go further and accept that the fact which he decides not to disclose either must be one which it was his duty to disclose, or must at least be one which he would ordinarily have disclosed in the normal course of his relationship with the claimant, but in the case of which he consciously decided to depart from what he would normally have done and to keep quiet about it". The argument boils down to whether the judge was entitled to find on the evidence that Mr Stevens and Ms Walker deliberately did not disclose that they were to receive payment for their work from another source to cover the cost of pursuing the claimant's case. The judge held that they knew, since it was obvious, that had they revealed the fact people in the position of the claimant would have questioned it. The defendant says that none of its witnesses was cross-examined upon this point at the trial. The defendant also complains that the judge rejected

its submission that in order to make these findings, the defendant ought to have had the opportunity to test the claimant's evidence in cross-examination.

42. I reject the defendant's submission so far as the claimant's own evidence was concerned. He was seriously ill, and the judge was entitled both to receive, and give appropriate weight to, his evidence, albeit it was not tested in cross examination. I have found more difficulty as regards the evidence of the defendant's witnesses. It is axiomatic that a claimant who wishes to rely on s 32(1) Limitation Act 1980 whether in relation to fraud, concealment or mistake, must fairly put the facts relied upon to the defendant's factual witnesses. Where, as here, the claimant argued that facts relevant to his right of action had been deliberately concealed from him by the defendant, this allegation had to be put to those witnesses called by the defendant whose behaviour was being called into account. Mr Glancy took me through his cross-examination of the defendant's witnesses to demonstrate that this was done. The allegation of deliberate concealment was not put, so far as I can see, in terms to the witnesses, but it was put that they had been misleading the claimant, on the basis that he thought that he had to pay to get his compensation, whereas the costs were being paid by the DTI. Mr Stevens was asked why that was not explained to him, and answered that it was not something that was hidden, and that claimants knew exactly what was happening. His evidence in this respect was rejected by the judge. It appears to me that the allegation that the claimant had been misled adequately put his case in relation to deliberate concealment, and I reject the defendant's complaint in this respect. In my view, the judge was entitled to make the findings he did on the evidence.

43. I consider that the limitation question was decided correctly in favour of the claimant, but this does not affect the outcome. For the reasons set out above, this appeal is dismissed.

Robert Glancy QC (instructed by Mishcon de Reya) appeared for the claimant.

James H Allen QC and *David Rose* (instructed by Brooke North LLP) appeared for the defendant.

Case 65
Earles

v

Barclays Bank plc

[2009] 6 Costs LR 906

Neutral Citation Number: [2009] EWHC 2500 (Mercantile)
High Court of Justice, Queen's Bench Division
8 October 2009

Before:
His Honour Judge Simon Brown QC
(sitting as an Additional High Court Judge)

Headnote

This appeal relates to a commercial dispute between a bank and one of its customers and was heavily dependent on the evidence and interpretation of the facts. For much of the time the claimant was unrepresented. The court determined that the Bank had achieved "success" but in an important costs judgment it limited its costs very severely on two main grounds; (i) conduct in relation to disclosure and electronic disclosure by the bank and (ii) proportionality. In particular, the court considered whether the application of City of London rates by the City of London firm in this matter which proceeded in the Birmingham Mercantile court were reasonable and ensured that the parties were on an equal footing.

Judgment

Introduction

1. This is the type of an action between a customer and his bank that has become increasingly prevalent in the mercantile court in these times following the recent economic downturn and the banking credit crisis.

2. The claimant is a customer of the defendant and has banked with them for over 30 years. Indeed, he is a former bank manager with the Bank, like his father before him. Subsequently, he became a property developer and is currently indebted to the Bank for some £2.45 million.

3. On 30 March 2005, Eden Holding Ltd ("the Company") was incorporated to sell beauty products in London through a team of salesmen led by Mr McKinney. The directors were the claimant and Mr McKinney. By 31 March 2006, the claimant's shareholding had increased from 20% and that of Mr McKinney reduced from 79%, according to the Directors Report and Financial statements for the year ended 31 March 2006. As a result they held equal shareholdings of 49% each. These accounts then showed a loss of £114,524 carried by shareholders funds in the same amount.

4. In April 2006, the claimant arranged a business loan for £75,000 to assist with capital expenditure on developing leasehold premises in Leamington Spa as a beauty salon. A business current account (a/c no: 8007–9782) was set up with an overdraft of £50,000 with statements to be sent monthly to the claimant's address. This overdraft had a £25,000 discretionary extra facility in the hands of the Relationship Manager without his need for recourse to the Bank's Credit Team. These potential liabilities were secured by a personal guarantee of £125,000 by the claimant that was in turn supported by a legal charge over a development site he owned personally called the Great Rollright site. The Relationship Manager for the Bank was Martin Leech aided by his assistants Katharine Shelley and Melanie Wigley-Jones of the Cardiff Business Centre Branch.

5. Concurrently, the claimant took out two separate loans of £600,000 and £625,000 to assist with construction work and "land" respectively relating to the development of a site at Great Rollright. A personal business account (2000–8990) was separately set up for the

claimant for this project in his name with statements being sent to him monthly at his home address.

6. Subsequently during 2006, substantial drawings on the Company account continued to be regularly made, mainly by cheques signed by Mr McKinney. During July, the overdraft leapt up and by July 17 at £129,695 it exceeded the level of the claimant's guarantee of £125,000. On July 19, £100,000 was transferred from the claimant's personal business account to reduce the overdraft to £32,260.30 i.e. below the £50,000 limit. This was the second leg of a two-part transaction, the first part being a drawdown of £100,000 from the Loan Account to the Personal Business Account. The claimant alleges that this was the first of five unauthorised transfers amounting to £265,000 between these accounts controlled by him.

7. On Tuesday 22 August 2006, a further drawdown of £100,000 was made from the Loan Account to the Personal Business Account. On the same day, £70,000 was transferred from the Personal Business Account to the Company Account. This brought the Company's overdraft down from £127,879.98 to £58,652.29 i.e. within the maximum discretionary limit of £75,000.

8. The third was on August 31 when £20,000 was transferred bringing it down from £92,564.16 to £74,918 i.e. just within the permissible maximum discretionary limit.

9. The fourth was shortly thereafter on September 7 when £50,000 was transferred bringing the Company's overdraft down from £105,674.62 to £59,244 i.e. again within the maximum discretionary limit of £75,000.

10. The fifth was on October 10 when £25,000 was transferred bringing the Company's overdraft down from £95,912.73 to £78,916.84 i.e. just above the maximum discretionary limit of £75,000. This arose because on 6 October 2006, upon receipt of a VAT refund of £75,000 into the Premier Account, £60,000 was transferred from the Premier Account to the Personal Business Account. On 10 October 2006, £25,000 was then transferred from the Personal Business Account to the Company Account.

11. The claimant subsequently resigned his position as director and as company secretary of the Company on 23 October 2006 and 2 January 2007 respectively.

12. On 1 August 2007 the banking affairs for the Company were transferred from the Relationship Manager and his team to the

Business Support department under Suzanne Parton. She held a meeting with the claimant and the Directors of the Company and resolved to obtain a report on the Company from BDO Stoy Hamlyn. Two days later, she says that the claimant notified her of unauthorised transfers of his personal monies into the Company account.

13. The BDO Report of 14 August 2007 detailed the parlous predicament of the Company. The transformation of the property had cost £400,000 against an initial budget of £250,000 financed primarily by directors' loans. The accounts showed an operating loss of £374,000 financed partly by management and partly by Bank financing.

14. Subsequently, the Company went into administration on 25 January 2008. The claimant is an unsecured creditor of the Company, pursuant to a written loan agreement dated 26 January 2007 which provided, amongst other matters, that the claimant would make available an unsecured loan to the Company of £324,425.88, that such sum represented the balance of his director's loan account as at the date of his resignation on 23 October 2006, and that the loan would be repaid over 36 monthly instalments beginning on 26 January 2008.

15. The claimant further alleges that as a result of the allegedly unauthorised transfers he has sustained consequential loss and damage. In October 2007, he claimed that his alleged consequential losses amounted to £605,000; a month later, in November 2007, he claimed that they had risen to nearly £1.1 million; by the time he issued this action, he was claiming that they were some £2,157,000. His total claim is now for some £2.4 million plus interest – approximately the same amount as he owes the Bank.

16. The Bank categorically denies that the disputed Transfers were not authorised by the claimant. It contends that the claimant gave oral telephone instructions to staff at the Bank's Cardiff Business Centre to make each of the Disputed Transfers, which the Bank was both entitled and obliged to follow in accordance with the terms and conditions governing the account. Without prejudice to that primary case, the Bank further contends that in any event the claim is excluded under the Condition 3 of the terms and conditions governing the account, and the claimant ratified and adopted the disputed transfers by entering into the Loan Agreement.

Issues at Trial

17. At the Case Management Conference on 12 June 2009, HHJ Kirkham ordered split trials in respect of the Bank's liability for breach of mandate and any entitlement to damages for breach of contract. Pursuant to the judge's order, the issues at this trial were therefore:

(1) Did Mr Earles authorise and instruct the Bank to process the Disputed Transfers (and each of them)? There is no longer any issue that these instructions could be given and accepted verbally by telephone or computer as Condition 3 of the Terms and Conditions governing the Personal Business account provide for such:

> "3.1 You can give us instructions verbally, in writing, by telephone or computer unless an additional condition limits the way in which instructions can be given.
>
> 3.2 Before we can accept instructions given to us by computer we will agree security procedures with you. ... We may also agree security procedures with you before accepting instructions given to us by telephone. ...
>
> 3.6 We can act on instructions (including instructions to make or collect payments from or into your account) given:
>
> (a) on a document bearing your signature(s); or
>
> (b) by telephone or computer, as long as we have followed the security procedures, whether or not the instruction was given by you; or
>
> (c) verbally, as long as we have been able to identify you without following the security procedures.
>
> As long as we have followed your instructions correctly, we can deduct the amount of any payment from your account. You agree that we may rely on any account number quoted in an instruction as the correct amount to be debited or credited."

The only issues are therefore purely factual: were these actually instructions given?

(2) Is the Bank entitled, in the events that occurred, to rely on Condition 9.4 of the Terms and Conditions to exclude Mr Earles' claim? This was abandoned by the Bank during the trial but the legal issue of ratification became live.

(3) Is the Bank entitled to rely on Condition 9.3 of the Terms and Conditions to exclude Mr Earles' claim for damages for breach of contract? Condition 9.3 provided:

> "We will not be liable to you in any circumstances for:
>
> Loss of business, loss of goodwill, loss of opportunity, loss of profit;
>
> Any type of special, consequential or indirect loss whatsoever."

Primary Issue

18. The resolution of the primary issue appears beguilingly simple. Were telephone calls or emails made on each of the five occasions and, if so, what was said or written?

19. Guidance to the fact finding judge on how to approach such a seemingly simple task has been given by judges of great eminence. The extra-judicial writing of Lord Bingham of Cornhill in a paper headed "The Judge as Juror: The Judicial Determination of Factual Issues" published in *The Business of Judging*, Oxford 2000, where it was reprinted from *Current Legal Problems*, vol. 38, 1985 p. 1–27 discusses the correct judicial approach:

> "Faced with a conflict of evidence on an issue substantially affecting the outcome of an action, often knowing that a decision this way or that will have momentous consequences on the parties' lives or fortunes, how can and should the judge set about his task of resolving it? How is he to resolve which witness is honest and which dishonest, which reliable and which unreliable? ...
>
> The normal first step in resolving issues of primary fact is, I feel sure, to add to what is common ground between the parties (which the pleadings in the action should have identified, but often do not) such facts as are shown to be incontrovertible. In many cases, letters or minutes written well before there was any breath of dispute between the parties may throw a very clear light on their knowledge and intentions at a particular time. In other cases, evidence of tyre marks, debris or where vehicles ended up may be crucial. To attach importance to matters such as these, which are independent of human recollection, is so obvious and standard a practice, and in some cases so inevitable, that no prolonged discussion is called for. It is nonetheless worth bearing in mind, when vexatious conflicts of oral testimony arise, that these fall to be judged against the background not only of what the parties agree to have

happened but also of what plainly did happen, even though the parties do not agree.

The most compendious statement known to me of the judicial process involved in assessing the credibility of an oral witness is to be found in the dissenting speech of Lord Pearce in the House of Lords in *Onassis* v *Vergottis* [1968] 2 Lloyds Rep 403 at p. 431. In this he touches on so many of the matters which I wish to mention that I may perhaps be forgiven for citing the relevant passage in full:

> '"Credibility" involves wider problems than mere "demeanour" which is mostly concerned with whether the witness appears to be telling the truth as he now believes it to be. Credibility covers the following problems. First, is the witness a truthful or untruthful person? Secondly, is he, though a truthful person telling something less than the truth on this issue, or though an untruthful person, telling the truth on this issue? Thirdly, though he is a truthful person telling the truth as he sees it, did he register the intentions of the conversation correctly and, if so has his memory correctly retained them? Also, has his recollection been subsequently altered by unconscious bias or wishful thinking or by over much discussion of it with others? Witnesses, especially those who are emotional, who think that they are morally in the right, tend very easily and unconsciously to conjure up a legal right that did not exist. It is a truism, often used in accident cases, that with every day that passes the memory becomes fainter and the imagination becomes more active. For that reason a witness, however honest, rarely persuades a judge that his present recollection is preferable to that which was taken down in writing immediately after the accident occurred. *Therefore, contemporary documents are always of the utmost importance.* [Emphasis added.] And lastly, although the honest witness believes he heard or saw this or that, is it so improbable that it is on balance more likely that he was mistaken? On this point it is essential that the balance of probability is put correctly into the scales in weighing the credibility of a witness. And motive is one aspect of probability. All these problems compendiously are entailed when a judge assesses the credibility of a witness; they are all part of one judicial process. And in the process contemporary documents and admitted or incontrovertible facts and probabilities must play their proper part.'

Every judge is familiar with cases in which the conflict between the accounts of different witnesses is so gross as to be inexplicable save on the basis that one or some of the witnesses are deliberately giving evidence which they know to be untrue ... more often dishonest evidence is likely to be prompted by the hope of gain, the desire to avert blame or criticism, or misplaced loyalty to one or other of the parties. The main tests needed to determine whether a witness is lying or not are, I think, the following, although their relative importance will vary widely from case to case:

(1) the consistency of the witness's evidence with what is agreed, or clearly shown by other evidence, to have occurred;

(2) the internal consistency of the witness's evidence;

(3) consistency with what the witness has said or deposed on other occasions;

(4) the credit of the witness in relation to matters not germane to the litigation;

(5) the demeanour of the witness.

The first three of these tests may in general be regarded as giving a useful pointer to where the truth lies. If a witness's evidence conflicts with what is clearly shown to have occurred, or is internally self-contradictory, or conflicts with what the witness has previously said, it may usually be regarded as suspect. It may only be unreliable, and not dishonest, but the nature of the case may effectively rule out that possibility.

The fourth test is perhaps more arguable."

20. Recently, fact finding judges have felt it useful to apply the following dictum of Lord Goff in *Grace Shipping* v *Sharp & Co* [1987] 1 Lloyd's Law Rep 207 at 215–6.

"And it is not to be forgotten that, in the present case, the judge was faced with the task of assessing the evidence of witnesses about telephone conversations which had taken place over five years before. In such a case, memories may very well be unreliable; and it is of crucial importance for the judge to have regard to the contemporary documents and to the overall probabilities. In this connection, their Lordships wish to endorse a passage from a judgment of one of their number in *Armagas*

Ltd v *Mundogas SA (The Ocean Frost)* [1985] 1 Lloyd's Rep 1, when he said at p. 57:

> 'Speaking from my own experience, I have found it essential in cases of fraud, when considering the credibility of witnesses, always to test their veracity by reference to the objective facts proved independently of their testimony, in particular by reference to the documents in the case, and also to pay particular regard to their motives and to the overall probabilities. It is frequently very difficult to tell whether a witness is telling the truth or not; and where there is a conflict of evidence such as there was in the present case, reference to the *objective facts and documents*, to the *witnesses' motives*, and to the *overall probabilities*, can be of very great assistance to a judge in ascertaining the truth. [Emphases added.]
>
> That observation is, in their Lordships' opinion, equally apposite in a case where the evidence of the witnesses is likely to be unreliable; and it is to be remembered that in commercial cases, such as the present, there is usually a substantial body of contemporary documentary evidence.'

In that context he was impressed by a witness described in the following terms.

> 'Although like the other main witnesses his evidence was a mixture of reconstruction and original recollection, he took considerable trouble to distinguish precisely between the two, to an extent which I found convincing and reliable.'

That is so important, and so infrequently done."

21. It is not realistic to expect any human beings to recall with any reliability what they said three years ago about run of the mill business transactions. Therefore it is crucial to follow the guidance of these very eminent jurists and in particular those emphasised regarding the analysis of contemporaneous documents; objective facts and documents; witnesses motives and overall probabilities. Since 2000 most key contemporaneous commercial documents are contained in Electronically Stored Information ("ESI") – today over 90% of communications are recorded in that form – phone records, texts, email, bank records etc. ESI are "documents" under the Civil Procedure Rules: CPR 31.4 and 31PD.2A. Accordingly, the rules for

"Standard Disclosure" apply: CPR 31.6. i.e. "only" those documents that are "supportive" or "adverse" to each party's cases. The abundance of this ESI in cyberspace means that potential litigants, in particular organisations such as Banks at the current time, need to anticipate having to give disclosure of specifically relevant electronic documentation and the means of doing so efficiently and effectively.

22. The claimant asserts that he queried the transfers for the first time at an unminuted meeting with Mr Leech and another in April 2007; this is denied by Mr Leech who recalls such a meeting the previous year but obviously no discussion about transfers that had not been made at that time.

23. The defendant alleges that the first time any of the transactions were queried was in a phone call on 3 August 2007 between Suzanne Parton and the claimant and that only related to three transactions £115,000. A fourth disputed transfer was undoubtedly only raised on 25 October 2007 by Lodders, solicitors acting on behalf of the claimant. The fifth was only raised at the opening of the trial – the defendants were relying on it in their witness statements served as being unchallenged. They contend this gives the lie to the claimant's case.

24. The claimant's solicitors, Lodders, wrote a letter before action and of complaint action to the Bank on 18 October 2007 claiming, *inter alia*, that: "The key issue in this matter relates to your Manager, Mr Martin Leech, making three separate transfers of funds globally totalling £115,000 from our client's business account to the account of Eden Holding limited."

25. The issues had crystallised and the likely resolution to them lay in the disclosure of respective emails and phone records of Mr Earles and Mr Leech (i.e. the Bank).

26. Beth Freeman, legal counsel to the Bank in the Barclays Legal & Compliance Section of GRCP Litigation responded on 19 October 2007 indicating that she would be "looking into the details surrounding your client's complaint and will provide a substantive response as soon as possible.".

27. Despite this none of the Bank, its legal department, the claimant or his solicitors took the obvious steps of preserving the contemporaneous phone and email records that would support or be adverse to their contentions and retaining them in anticipation of

litigation between them – "litigation hold" as it is termed in US under their Federal Rules of Civil Procedure.

28. However, in this jurisdiction as in Australia, there is no duty to preserve documents prior to the commencement of proceedings: *British American Tobacco Australia Services Ltd* v *Cowell* [2002] VSCA 197, a decision approved in this country by Morritt VC in *Douglas* v *Hello* [2003] EWHC 55 at [86]. However, the leading text book in this area – *Documentary Evidence* by Charles Hollander QC – suggests in para 10-06 of the 10th edition that "there might be cases where it was appropriate to draw adverse inferences from a party's conduct before the commencement of proceedings". In my judgment there would have to be some clear evidence of deliberate spoliation in anticipation of litigation before one could legitimately draw evidential "adverse inferences" in those circumstances. There is no such evidential basis in this case.

29. After the commencement of proceedings the situation is radically different. In *Woods* v *Martins Bank Ltd* [1959] 1 QB 55 at 60, Salmon J said: "It cannot be too clearly understood that solicitors owe a duty to the court, as officers of the court to make sure, as far as possible, that no relevant documents have been omitted from their client's list."

30. In the case of documents not preserved after the commencement of proceedings then the defaulting party risk "adverse inferences" being drawn for such "spoliation": *Infabricks Ltd* v *Jaytex Ltd* [1985] FSR 75.

31. Contrary to CPR 31PD.2A, there were no pre-Case Management Conference discussions about the disclosure of any of this key Electronically Stored Information ("ESI"). There was no apparent discussion about it at the Case Management Conference on June 12, no Costs Management of the disclosure process despite the Costs Management Pilot Scheme in operation at the Birmingham Mercantile Court for the Jackson Review on Costs and no order made in respect of it. Order 4 provided without any particularity "the parties shall give standard disclosure by list (confined to Liability Issues) pursuant to CPR 31.6 no later than 4.00 pm on 6 July 2009 with inspection by provision of copy documents 7 days notice".

32. The list dated 13 July 2009 produced by Elizabeth Freeman, In house Legal counsel for the defendant, verified a search for electronic documents. These did not include telephone records of the Bank and

Mr Leech that might have verified calls received from the claimant's mobile telephone number 07813 211849 that was given as the contact details in his application forms to the Bank. The list does not include any "pink and yellow" Transfer Sheets to record instructions received from customers over the phone or verbally according to para 53 of Katharine Shelley's witness statement. These documents would clearly be relevant for the purposes of CPR 31.6. The explanation given by counsel for the bank in closing submissions for this gross omission is that it was decided that they were of marginal relevance and it would be disproportionate to undertake a task that might take a team working for three months! I simply do not accept that assessment. In the light of the fact that the Bank has incurred over £154,000 in costs in defending this claim for £2.45m and that the documents would clearly have assisted the case in determining whether the oral authorisations were given, I reject both those submissions. However, I accept that these were the reasons, albeit poor ones, and that it was not due to the Bank's deliberate hiding of them; otherwise the witness statement prepared for Katharine Shelley would simply not have referred to them.

33. The search also revealed that the emails and electronic documents of all Bank employees had been searched and retrieved but the critical ones of Mr Leech's email account had not been found with an explanation that he was no longer an employee of the Bank. However, during closing submissions I was told by counsel for the Bank that she was instructed that Mr Leech had been asked in 2007 if he had any relevant emails on his laptop and he had said no. This does not appear on the disclosure statement in 2009. During this time and right until shortly before trial, the claimant was unrepresented. On 30 July 2009 Simmons & Simmons, the solicitors acting for the Bank wrote to the claimant demanding proper disclosure of his records correctly stating: "Disclosure of documents is not optional. It is a crucial element of civil litigation". It then threatens an application with draconian consequences of a strike out of the Claim before going on to say "It should also include your personal telephone bills for the period of the disputed transfers, which will be relevant to the question of whether you made the telephone calls to the bank on relevant dates." A similar retort would have been made against the defendant if the claimant had been legally represented. These matters should have been raised at the CMC: see CPD 31 PD 2A.

34. The claimant responded on 1 August 2009 by stating in an email that he had undertaken appropriate searches but that "Phone bills have not survived from this period and anyway I did not receive itemised bills. I have never been given the dates or times that Barclays claim they spoke to someone on the telephone nor what process of identification was asked for or given".

35. Both parties now submit that the court should draw "adverse inferences" against the other party for their failure to disclose their own telephone records on and just before each of the alleged transactions that would establish one way or another whether the claimant and Mr Leech had been in telephone contact with one another at that time – the claimant vigorously denying he had; Mr Leech swearing to the contrary. Furthermore with the claimant denying he was in any form of regular telephone contact with anyone at the Bank about the state of his accounts and with Mr Leech and both his assistants swearing that he was constantly in contact, then all the Bank's phone records for these personnel were also highly relevant to the key issue.

36. None of this documentation has been disclosed, nor have the Transfer Sheets and no relevant emails between Mr Leech and the claimant during this period have emerged that might have shed valuable light on what the respective individuals did or [did not] believe before the spectre of litigation loomed.

37. In cases where there is a deliberate void of evidence, such negativity can be used as a weapon in adversarial litigation to fill the evidential gap and so establish a positive case. In *British Railways Board v Herrington* [1972] 1 AER 786, Lord Diplock stated:

> "The appellants, who are a public corporation, elected to call no witnesses, thus depriving the court of any positive evidence as to whether the condition of the fence and the adjacent terrain had been noticed by any particular servant of theirs or as to what he or any other of their servants either thought or did about it. This is a legitimate tactical move under our adversarial system of litigation. But a defendant who adopts it cannot complain if the court draws from the facts which have been disclosed all reasonable inferences as to what are the facts which the defendant has chosen to withhold.
>
> A court may take judicial notice that railway lines are regularly patrolled by linesman and gangers. In the absence of evidence to the contrary, it is

entitled to infer that one or more of them in the course of several weeks noticed what was plain for all to see. Anyone of common sense would realise the danger that the state of the fence so close to the live rail created for little children coming to the meadow to play. As the appellants elected to call none of the persons who patrolled the line there is nothing to rebut the inference that they did not lack the common sense to realise the danger. A court is accordingly entitled to infer from the inaction of the appellants that one or more of their employees decided to allow the risk to continue of some child crossing the boundary and being injured or killed by the live rail rather than to incur the trivial trouble and expense of repairing the gap in the fence."

38. In *India Oil Corporation* v *Greenstone Shipping SA* [1988] 1 QB 345 per Staughton J the court discussed the modern meaning of the rule of evidence known in Latin as "omnia praesumuntur contra spoliatorem" (everything is presumed against a destroyer (of evidence) – "spoliation" as it is termed in US and which the rule of "litigation hold" is designed to combat:

"If the wrongdoer prevents the innocent party proving how much of his property has been taken, then the wrongdoer is liable to the greatest extent possible in the circumstances."

39. This presumption was used in the case of *Infabrics Ltd* v *Jaytex Ltd* (*supra*).

40. In my judgment, the deficiencies of disclosure on the part of the claimant, a litigant in person during the disclosure process, are probably due to his lack of appreciation of the Civil Procedure Rules. I accept that by 2009 he had lost his mobile phone records and, as a litigant in person at the time, he would have found it difficult to get his service provider to find back up records. It would therefore be wrong to make any adverse inferences against him on that score.

41. The lack of disclosure by the Bank of the phone records, the Transfer Sheets and email account of Mr Leech cannot be ascribed to a lack of understanding of the duties of disclosure and how to procure retrieval of electronic "documents" by the Bank's first class legal teams, both in and out house, and document storage managers as demonstrated by the correspondence referred to above. The explanation that the void occurred because Mr Leech had retired from the Bank's employment is a lame excuse – an expert in information

technology, either in house or a consultant, could easily have been instructed to retrieve ESI from various back up sources one would have thought but no such expert appears to have been instructed to do so. One expects a major high street Bank in this day and age of electronic records and communication with an in house litigation department to have an efficient and effective information management system in place to provide identification, preservation, collection, processing, review analysis and production of its ESI in the disclosure process in litigation and regulation. However, even though the failure to disclose such critical information to assist the court is surprising and to be deplored, there is no evidence that it has been done deliberately or constitutes spoliation in order to gain a tactical evidential advantage at the trial. None of the Bank's personnel such as in house counsel Elizabeth Freeman who undertook the bank's disclosure have been challenged on that. Accordingly, I decline to make any adverse inferences against the Bank either. The Bank's telephone databases and back up tapes as well as the Transfer Sheets should have been disclosed but I do not believe it has been established that these have been deliberately withheld to avoid its own case being undermined. In my judgment this was a decision made by the Bank's legal team on the erroneous grounds of relevance and proportionality, not as part of any tactical move to gain an evidential advantage in the litigation.

42. The evidence that I am left with in the 500 page bundle of trial documents is primarily that of the witnesses themselves and the contemporaneous Credit Call Reports of Mr Leech's assistants, Katharine Shelley and Melanie Wigley-Jones.

43. Mr Earles provided a short very general statement as his evidence in chief. I found his answers in cross examination to be unfocussed, vague and evasive, even though the issues he had to deal with were simple. I found his answers that, as a former bank manager and a businessman running various large property developing projects on his own and a company's account, he did not look at the bank statements sent to him, quite incredible. On the other hand I found Mr Leech to be an impressive witness. Like all the Bank's witnesses, the presentation of their witness statements was a model but that is primarily due to the drafting no doubt done with the considerable assistance of their instructed litigation solicitors. This practice of drafting of witness statements and their substitution for evidence in chief makes evaluation of witnesses' evidence on the issue of credibility

more difficult. However, in oral evidence under strenuous cross examination he was clear in his recollections, well reasoned and emotionally detached – he is no longer working for the Bank. He had worked for 30 years in the Bank since he joined immediately after leaving school working his way up to a position of high standing. Whereas Mr Earles has an obvious motive to say the transactions were unauthorised on account of his undisputed indebtedness to the Bank, Mr Leech has not such motive – he is no longer employed by the Bank and he was under no pressure from the Bank or the Credit Team at any time. He was simply trying to help the claimant manage his various customers' accounts within the limits provided by the Credit Team.

44. Similarly, I found Katharine Shelley and Melanie Wigley-Jones (Suzanne Parton too) to be impressive witnesses all with lengthy experience in working in the Bank following precise routines and procedures. In particular, I find that I can place great reliance on their contemporaneous Credit Call Reports and their evidence that Mr Earles maintained close and watchful control over the operation of both his own and the Company's accounts, telephoning most mornings to check the balances on the accounts, discuss funds that he expected to be paid into the accounts, and identify how he intended to utilise those funds once received. The undisclosed phone records of the Bank and of the claimant's mobile telephone would have conclusively proved this. However, in my judgment this is what would be expected of a businessman personally involved in juggling his finances upon risky property developments. As a former bank manager, I simply do not believe he would abandon that task to his Relationship Manager who had no stake in how the developments funded by Mr Earles personally turned out. His only interest was in maintaining the accounts within their various prescribed limits; he would have no interest in how the developments would profit – such was Mr Earles' concern.

45. The Credit Call Reports clearly demonstrate the instructions between Mr Leech and to his assistants. Apart from one they do not expressly record actual communications with the claimant. Crucially, one of them on 27 September 2006 recorded by Katharine Shelley records "spoke with customer" i.e. Mr Earles. The other reports merely summarise such as "customer has instructed us" on October 4. In my judgment, these records support the Bank's case that all transactions followed the instructions given by the customer.

46. Mr Earles' business accounts and the Company account were all opened by him and held at the Bank's Cardiff Business Centre branch. Mr Earles was the first point of contact for the Company Account; its main business/organisation address and correspondence address was Mr Earles' home address; and the monthly bank statements for the Company were sent to Mr Earles' home address. He had all the details to be able to monitor the accounts closely.

47. Furthermore, a fourth disputed transfer was undoubtedly only raised on 25 October 2007 by Lodders, solicitors acting on behalf of the claimant. If this had been a genuinely disputed transfer then in my judgment it would have been raised when the other three were on 3 August 2007. A fifth "disputed transaction" of £50,000 was only first raised in an application to amend the particulars of claim on the morning of the trial on 28 September 2009 i.e. just over three years later when all the documents had long been disclosed and it became apparent to the claimant from the recently served witness statements of the defendants that they were relying on this transfer being an unchallenged one of a similar type to the disputed ones as a QED of their case. In my judgment, the claimant challenged that transfer because he realised that otherwise his case was completely undermined. If there had been any true dispute about that transaction, then, in my judgment, it would have been raised far sooner by such a savvy businessman as the claimant.

48. I reject Mr Earles' evidence that he met Mr Leech in April 2007 with a prospective purchaser of the Great Rollright development. I prefer the evidence of Mr Leech on this. The meeting was in April 2006 before the transactions came into being. If the meeting had been in 2007 and the transfers discussed then I would have expected details to have appeared in the Credit Call Reports that were diligently maintained.

49. The Bank's records demonstrate, and the Bank's witnesses confirm, that throughout this period Mr Earles gave repeated assurances to the Bank that financing/funding would very soon be received into the Company Account to reduce the Company's significant and excessive indebtedness, but ultimately no such funds were in fact forthcoming. However, as the Company Account statements and cheques drawn demonstrate, the Company needed to make substantial ongoing payments to its suppliers and contractors. Without the Disputed Transfers and the Undisputed Transfer, items

presented for payment on the Company Account would have been returned and the Company thus unable to operate its bank account and pay for its refurbishment works.

50. In my judgment it is clear that the reason why the claimant transferred monies into the Company Account was because throughout the relevant period the Company was operating the Account significantly in excess of the borrowing facilities extended to it by the Bank; had substantial outgoings that it needed to meet; did not manage to obtain further financing elsewhere (notwithstanding Mr Earles' repeated assurances that such funds would be forthcoming); and regularly reached the point where the Bank would cease allowing payments out of the Eden Account if additional funds were not put into it.

51. The documentary evidence therefore demonstrates, and the Bank's witnesses strongly confirm, that Mr Earles made good and frequent use of telephone access to the Business Centre staff, including for the purpose of giving instructions to make transfers. Mr Earles does not contend that other transfers made on telephone instructions – self-evidently without his giving signed authorisation and/or ID verification – were unauthorised.

52. Mr Earles' assertion that he had only ever spoken to any of the Business Centre team briefly is implausible and contrary to the contemporaneous evidence which I accept as accurate. The Company Account appeared very frequently on the Business Centre's daily "refer lists" of accounts that had exceeded their specified overdraft limit. The appearance of an account on the refer list had serious consequences, including review and possible rejection of items presented or payments requested from the account; if the excess were not remedied within a fairly short space of time, referral to the Bank's credit committee; and ultimately, if the excess still continued, withdrawal of banking facilities altogether. As one would expect, customers whose accounts appeared on the refer list therefore quickly found themselves in discussions with Mr Leech, Katharine Shelley and Melanie Wigley-Jones about when and how the customer proposed to bring the account back within the specified overdraft limit. Mr Earles was the first point of contact on the Eden Account and finance director of the Company; given the extent to which Eden operated in excess of its agreed borrowing facilities, it is simply not credible for Mr Earles to claim that he had only ever spoken to any of the Business Centre team briefly.

53. There is no plausible explanation as to why, on his own case, he apparently failed to notice these transactions.

54. On 31 July 2007, Mr Earles' and the Company's accounts were transferred to the Bank's Business Support Unit under the management of Suzanne Parton. She promptly called an urgent meeting on 1 August 2007 with Mr Earles and representatives of the Company to discuss its dire financial position, at which she explained that the Bank could not provide further funding, and that the Company was likely to fail without an injection of capital. In that event, the Bank would of course call upon Mr Earles' guarantee. Two days later, Mr Earles telephoned Suzanne Parton to say that he wanted to bring something else to her attention, namely that £115,000 of his personal money had been transferred from one of his accounts to the Company Account without his authority. When asked why he had not raised the matter until now, Mr Earles then claimed that he had previously complained about these transfers (the Second, Third and Fourth Disputed Transfers) by telephone. There is no record of this and if the bank had been advised of that then I am certain they would have noted such matters and taken appropriate action.

55. In my judgment, the first occasion on which Mr Earles complained about the Second, Third and Fifth Disputed Transfers was following the meeting on 1 August 2007. I reject his evidence that he raised any issue about unauthorised transfers at any meeting with Mr Leech in April 2007. If he had then I am certain Mr Leech and Mr Earles would both have taken action about that.

56. As to Mr Earles' "discovery" of the First Disputed Transfer, his explanation in this regard is bizarre. It was not until 25 October 2007, over 15 months after the event, that Mr Earles complained about the First Disputed Transfer, in a letter from his solicitors. His explanation for not noticing this transfer when he reviewed his bank statements (which on his own case had happened well before this date) was that it had coincided with the transfer into the Account of £100,000 from the Loan Account and therefore the balance on the account was not affected. It is simply not credible for Mr Earles to assert that he failed to notice any of the receipts set out on his account statement, let alone a receipt of such a substantial sum as £100,000, or that the balance was (on his own case, given that he does not dispute that the drawdown was authorised) £100,000 less than he would have

expected; nor indeed is it credible that he did not notice the payment on the statement for the Company Account.

57. In my judgment, the contemporaneous documentation, the objective facts and documents, witnesses' motives and the overall probabilities all support the clear evidence of the bank officials running these accounts that these transactions were orally authorised by the claimant. I believe Mr Leech and I disbelieve Mr Earles.

58. Accordingly, I find for the Bank on Issue 1 and the claim must fail.

The Secondary issue

59. This is now strictly otiose in the light of the above finding but I will briefly deal with it. In my judgment such a term is entirely reasonable where a Bank is seeking to operate a commercial customer's various business accounts within their prescribed limits. It would be unfair on a Bank to impose upon it liability for the potential losses of a highly speculative property developer juggling with funds in order to make himself substantial profits whilst being exposed to potential losses. The Bank was undertaking no similar risks for profit. It was merely providing facilities and assumed no further duties of care that would give rise to consequential losses: they did not fall within the scope of the risk. However, if such duties were established and breaches established, then, in my judgment, it was entirely reasonable for the Bank to limit the commercial consequences for any defaults in the provision of their services to commercial customers, such as the claimant (a former Bank Manager and property developer) with an equal bargaining power in the competitive financial services market. The Bank has discharged its duty to establish that their conditions were fair under the Unfair Contract Terms Act.

The Tertiary Issue

60. Again this is strictly otiose. In the Loan Agreement entered into between Mr Earles and the Company on 26 January 2007, Mr Earles confirmed that the total sum owing to him by the Company representing the balance of his director's loan account as at the date of his resignation on 23 October 2006, was £324,425.88. This balance included the Disputed Transfers: Mr Earles has confirmed that in the Loan Agreement "Eden Holding just reflected the fact that [the Bank] had sent funds to them from my account".

61. Thus even assuming that Mr Earles did not authorise the

Disputed Transfers, Mr Earles ratified and adopted them by entering into the Loan Agreement: see *London Intercontinental Trust Ltd* v *Barclays Bank Ltd* [1980] 1 Lloyd's Rep 241.

62. In entering into the Loan Agreement, Mr Earles thereby expressly recognised that the Company was indebted to him in the sum of £324,425.88, which debt *included* the Disputed Transfers. This confirms my earlier finding on the primary issue. That recognition would be wholly inconsistent with Mr Earles having any claim against the Bank on the basis that the Disputed Transfers were unauthorised. Either he had a claim against the Company, or he had a claim against the Bank; he did not have a claim against both.

Costs

63. The defendant has been "successful" in its defence of the Claim. Accordingly, under CPR 44.3 it is *prima facie* entitled to its costs against the "unsuccessful" claimant.

64. This has been a short trial of essentially a very simple factual issue with five witnesses and 500 pages of documents (mostly irrelevant – about 10% relevance) lasting just two days plus short oral submissions. The claimant was only represented until the proceedings began and again shortly before trial. He is heavily indebted to the defendant in the sum of £2.45m. It therefore seemed just to assess the costs summarily rather than send them for potentially expensive "detailed assessment".

65. The claimant's cost schedule is therefore rather modest at £22,003.75 and the rates charged are within costs guidelines.

66. The defendant's costs amount to £202,480.50. The panel arrangement agreed with the Bank and its litigation lawyers is that each phase of litigation is budget capped. Accordingly, £48,409.25 is above the budget cap and is being borne by the defendants' solicitors. £154,071.25 is now sought for dealing with these short preliminary issues concerning five transactions amounting to £265,000. One point was abandoned by the successful bank but I am satisfied that it had little costs involved.

67. I have been critical of the "conduct" by the Bank of its disclosure and its electronic disclosure.

68. As regards disclosure, the Bank failed to give disclosure of the Transfer Sheets referred to in para 53 of the witness statement of Katharine Shelley. They were clearly relevant under the narrow test of

CPR 31.6 to the primary issue in the case. The very fact that they were referred to in the carefully crafted witness statement proves that and it ought to have been obvious to the defendants' lawyers. Their absence made the task of the court immeasurably harder to the extent that it considered lengthy submission as to whether or [not] to draw adverse inferences against the Bank itself. I am satisfied that it was a decision of the legal team on the erroneous grounds of disproportionality.

69. As regards electronic disclosure, the Bank, through its in-house counsel, Elizabeth Freeman, should have procured and retained Mr Leech's email account and phone records for the period covered by the three transactions questioned in the letter before action from Lodders dated 18 October 2007. In house counsel should not have simply accepted Mr Leech's word that there were no relevant emails. His laptop should have been retained in 2007 and certainly ascertained upon his leaving the Bank in November 2008. This earlier non disclosure of the email records should have featured in the disclosure statement. It is accepted that it was strictly under no procedural duty to do so in civil procedure law. However, "conduct" before proceedings can be taken into account in dealing with costs under CPR 44.3(5).

70. Secondly, the Bank's litigation lawyers should have "discussed" with the claimant well "prior to the case management conference" the electronic disclosure of both Mr Earles and Mr Leech's phone and email records as expressly provided by CPR 31PD.2A2 . It did neither but did rehearse the issue of disclosure with the claimant two years later in August 2009 shortly before trial. This was far too late with the result that the witnesses and the court have had to deal with a case with critical contemporaneous documents missing. This is contrary to the Overriding Objective of "ensuring" that the case is "dealt with expeditiously and fairly".

71. It might be contended that CPR 31PD 2A and electronic disclosure are little known or practised outside the Admiralty and Commercial Court. If so, such myth needs to be swiftly dispelled when over 90% of business documentation is electronic in form. The Practice Direction is in the Civil Procedure Rules and those practising in civil courts are expected to know the rules and practise them; it is *gross* incompetence not to.

72. This is long established. In *Fletcher & Son* v *Jubb, Booth & Helliwell* [1920] 1 KB 275 at page 280, Scrutton LJ approved a

passage from a judgment of Tindal CJ in *Godefroy v Dalton* (1830) 6 Bing 460:

> "It would be extremely difficult to define the exact limit by which the skill and diligence which an attorney undertakes to furnish in the conduct of a cause is bounded or to trace precisely the dividing line between the reasonable skill and diligence which appears to satisfy his undertaking, and the crass negligentia or lata culpa mentioned in some of the cases, for which he is undoubtedly responsible. The cases, however, which have been cited and commented on at the bar, appear to establish, in general, that *he is liable for the consequences of ignorance or non-observance of the rules of practice of this court*; for the want of care in the preparation of the cause for trial; or of the attendance thereon with his witnesses and for the mismanagement of so much of the conduct of a cause as is usually and ordinarily allotted to his department of the profession." (emphasis added)

73. As regards "disclosure" (and this includes electronic disclosure), it is worth repeating here what was said in *Woods v Martins Bank Ltd* [1959] 1 QB 55 at 60, where Salmon J said: "It cannot be too clearly understood that solicitors owe a duty to the court, as officers of the court to make sure, as far as possible, that no relevant documents have been omitted from their client's list."

74. The disclosure of only the key documents in a case is absolutely *essential* to a court if it is to achieve the accurate and efficient fact finding sought by the parties to civil litigation.

75. In my judgment, the "conduct" of electronic disclosure by the Bank and its lawyers fell far below the standards to be expected of those practicing in the civil courts and I am going to take that into account under CPR 44.3 in the award of costs to the successful party.

76. In my judgment, if disclosure of these records had taken place two years ago on August 2007, there was a reasonable prospect that this matter would not have proceeded to trial and so incurred the legal costs it has. The Bank's case, on my judgment, would have been unanswerable but of course the claimant's attitude may have been to ignore that. However, if the documents had been disclosed then a Summary Judgment application might well have been successful.

77. In my judgment, there were reasonable prospects of saving the main body of these itemised costs which are mainly those for trial but I accept that the additional work on proper disclosure would have

added to the itemised bill before me. In my judgment, a fair assessment of this would be to award the successful party 50% of its costs against the unsuccessful claimant.

78. Secondly, the Schedule of Costs of the defendants in my judgment is "disproportionate" to the sums and issues involved in what was only a simple factual trial on preliminary issues involving five witnesses and, in reality 50 or so pages of documents, and no issues of law or construction of contract.

79. I accept that the Bank is entitled to instruct the very best City of London firms (as Simmons & Simmons undoubtedly are) and counsel from leading commercial chambers as Fountain Court in London undoubtedly are too. I also welcome such excellent representation in the Mercantile Court in Birmingham as it makes the task of judging much easier when good preparation and advocacy is displayed.

80. However, in making what is a "costs transference" order, in my judgment the sum to be ordered to be transferred must objectively be a reasonable one for the unsuccessful party to bear. The overriding objective requires the court to observe "proportionality" and to "ensure that the parties are on an equal footing". Here we have an impecunious bank customer facing the might of one of the country's largest banks and a blue chip legal team to match when he has struggled to afford to have a highly competent but small firm from Stratford upon Avon to represent him just for the trial. Ordinary citizens must have proper access to civil justice without the fear of exclusion by the prospect that they will face paying for the exorbitance of their adversary should they be unsuccessful in their litigation.

81. Many other banks who come before the Mercantile Court on similar cases, such as HSBC, use in house legal teams only and able solicitor advocates charging similar rates as Lodders (solicitors for the claimant here) that lie within the Birmingham cost Guidelines.

82. In my judgment, it is only fair and just that the bill of costs adopts rates similar to those and not top class City of London rates – this is not the type of case that merits those. In my judgment this halves the rates – a London partner charging £420–£425 is half that here at the maximum Birmingham rates of £217. It is simply not acceptable to sanction rates of £235 to £250 per hour for an Assistant Solicitor admitted to the Roll in March 2008 when the Birmingham Cost Guideline rates for Inner Ring senior partners at the top firms is "only" £217. In my judgment, this case was tried in the Birmingham

Mercantile Court by choice of the claimant and the defendant agreed with this (the defendant normally having the right to request venue at its registered address – here London: CPR 26.2 and (2) & 30.3(2)). In those circumstances, I believe it is just that Birmingham rates, not City of London rates, prevail.

83. Again comparison of counsel's fees shows a discrepancy between counsel from St Phillips of Birmingham for the claimant (2001 call) of £6,195 for three day trial and £18,400 for counsel (2002 call) for the defendant from Fountain Court of London. I accept that counsel for the defendant was briefed earlier and had more preparation time. I would like to stress that both performed to a very high and helpful standard but I do believe that the sum of £18,400 is far too high for this case and half that is reasonable in all the circumstances.

84. On the question of hours spent, I am prepared to accept the hours worked. However, these hours seem excessive for what is quite a simple case. 41 hours on dealing with Statements of Case and a mind boggling 223.1 hours in dealing with the defendant's evidence of five witnesses and 500 pages of documents is far too much. However, I take into account that this is leavened by the fact that these excesses have been borne by the defendant's solicitors thereby cutting it down to what was deemed reasonable by the Bank itself when it set its budget cap. I therefore accept the hours being charged for and sought against the unsuccessful claimant.

85. It would, however, have been much more preferable if Costs Management had been applied during Case Management and at the Case Management Conference as per the pilot scheme in this court as part of the Review of Costs in Civil Proceedings by Lord Justice Jackson. This would have controlled the costs before they were actually spent. The defendant was facing a litigant in person for much of this action and that places a very onerous burden on the opposition to fairly and diligently prepare the case for trial. Not many litigants in person appreciate that when they are spending nothing on legal services themselves but only vicariously so riding everything on the result vis-à-vis costs as well as the outcome of the action.

86. Accordingly, in my judgment, the fair award of costs is that the unsuccessful claimant should pay the successful defendant 25% of its Schedule of Costs (including VAT) amounting to £38,517.81 – a sum that is proportionate and fair.

Case 66
Kris Motor Spares Ltd
v
Fox Williams LLP

[2009] 6 Costs LR 931

Neutral Citation Number: [2009] EWHC 2813 (QB)
High Court of Justice, Queen's Bench Division
13 November 2009

Before:
Holroyde J (sitting with assessors:
Master Wright and Mr Simon Veysey)

Headnote

The judge, hearing an appeal from a decision of a costs judge who had heard conflicting oral evidence, and made clear findings thereon, affirmed the general principle that much respect should be paid to such findings, but also dealt at length with the detailed criticisms of the costs judge's reserved judgment that had been advanced during the hearing of the appeal.

Judgment

1. **HOLROYDE J:** This is an appeal by Kris Motor Spares Ltd ("KMS") against a judgment given by Costs Judge Master Rogers on 6 February 2009 refusing KMS's application for a detailed assessment of the bill of costs delivered by their former solicitors Fox Williams LLP ("FW").

2. I begin by summarising what I regard as the principal features of the factual background to KMS's application and appeal. I do so as

briefly as possible, and deliberately omit matters which do not seem to me to be relevant to my judgment. It is however necessary to go into a little detail, in view of the criticisms which KMS make of Master Rogers' judgment, including in particular their attack on his findings of fact.

3. KMS is owned and controlled by Mr Krishnani, an experienced and successful businessman. So too, as I understand it, is another company called Reachbyte Ltd ("Reachbyte") KMS and Reachbyte engaged in a substantial level of share trading through stockbrokers Brewin Dolphin Securities Ltd and Brewin Nominees Ltd (collectively, for convenience, "BD"). KMS and Reachbyte appointed a Mrs Mehta (an employee of Reachbyte) to conduct this share trading on their behalf. It was alleged that Mrs Mehta acted dishonestly, and that one or more employees of BD acted in collusion with her. In particular, it was alleged that daily records of trading were falsified, and a false picture given to KMS and Reachbyte of the profitability of their share trading. Those allegations led to substantial litigation commencing in 2002 between KMS and Reachbyte, and BD ("the BD litigation"). Mrs Mehta became one of a number of parties to that litigation. The solicitors acting for BD were Barlow Lyde and Gilbert ("BLG").

4. Over the course of the BD litigation, KMS and Reachbyte jointly used at least three different firms of solicitors before FW were engaged. I am concerned with KMS, and will therefore for the most part refer only to that company.

5. At one stage of the litigation KMS were represented by solicitors Sibley & Co, but in about July 2004 they became dissatisfied with the work of that firm and withdrew their instructions. The dissatisfaction gave rise to allegations of negligence and a dispute over the fees of Sibley & Co (collectively, "the Sibley litigation"). It is not necessary to go into any detail about the Sibley litigation, save to say that there came a stage when there had to be a detailed assessment of the fees which Sibley & Co had charged to KMS.

6. KMS were next represented by DKLL solicitors. However, both those solicitors and KMS came to the view that a larger firm should take over conduct of the litigation, and there was an amicable parting of the ways. At that stage KMS instructed FW. They did so because FW had been recommended to Mr Krishnani by Mr Tony Craze, a retired stockbroker and radio commentator, from whom Mr Krishnani had sought advice in connection with the litigation.

7. It was necessary in the course of the BD litigation for KMS to adduce expert evidence as to stockbroking practices. Mr Craze had apparently been Mr Krishnani's preferred choice as an expert witness in that regard, but he had declined to act in that capacity. He had however recommended as an expert a Mr John Symes, who was engaged by KMS some time before FW were instructed – I think in about 2004 – and who prepared a number of reports. Mr Craze himself was also involved from about 2004 in advising and assisting Mr Krishnani in relation to the litigation, describing his role as "case manager". It seems that he and Mr Symes had complementary areas of expertise, in that Mr Craze was particularly knowledgeable about "front office" aspects of stockbroking, whilst Mr Symes' expertise related to "back office" matters. Both gentlemen received their remuneration from Mr Krishnani rather than from any of the solicitors instructed to represent KMS.

8. It follows that both Mr Craze and Mr Symes were working in connection with the BD litigation, and being paid by Mr Krishnani, long before FW became involved. Before the Master there was an issue as to what exactly FW were told about the arrangements between Mr Krishnani on the one hand, and Messrs Craze and Symes on the other hand. I refer below to a particular issue relating to a lunch meeting in July 2006.

9. FW agreed to act for KMS and Reachbyte on a conditional fee basis. The conditional fee agreement ("CFA") was signed on 29 March 2006. The essence of the agreement was that FW were to employ named persons (of differing levels of seniority) to work on the case at specified hourly rates: these persons included Mr Greager, Mr Dykins and Miss Roake. FW's ordinary fees were calculated by reference to those hourly rates. In the event of KMS being successful in the litigation, FW would be paid their ordinary fees plus an uplift of 30%. If KMS were unsuccessful, FW's fees would be limited to 70% of their ordinary fees. This was the first time FW had worked on a conditional fee basis, and the CFA was specifically drafted for the occasion.

10. It is appropriate to go into more detail about the relevant terms of the CFA which was made between Reachbyte Ltd and KMS Ltd ("the Clients"), and FW. Clauses 1 and 2 identified what work was and was not covered. Clause 3.1 said that FW's fees were calculated by reference to the hourly rates set out in clause 5. Clause 3 then continued, in part, as follows:

"3.2 FW has agreed to act for the Clients on the basis that it will charge the Clients for all of its own work at a discounted hourly rate in the event that the Clients lose all of the Claims but it will charge its ordinary hourly rate in the event that the Clients win the Claims together with a Success Fee

3.3 If the Clients lose the Claims, FW agrees to charge the Clients its own legal fees calculated at 70% of the hourly rates set out in Cl 5. These will form the Non-Conditional Fees ...

3.4 FW will render monthly interim invoices on account of costs to the Clients for sums not more than the amount of the Non-Conditional Fees ... together with 'Disbursement only' invoices, and those invoices will be payable within 14 days of receipt ...

3.5 If the Clients win the Claims FW will charge its own legal fees at the full hourly rates (100% of the hourly rates) set out in Cl 5 below, hereby referred to as the Ordinary Fees. In addition FW will charge the Clients a Success Fee calculated in accordance with Cl 7 below.

3.6 The difference between the amount of the Non-Conditional Fees and the Ordinary Fees will form the Conditional Fees."

11. By Clause 7.1, "The success fee shall be 100% of the conditional fees". Thus the effect of the agreement was that if the clients lost, FW would only be paid 70% of their ordinary fees; but if the clients won, FW would be paid 130% of their ordinary fees.

12. Clause 8 confirmed that the effect of the CFA had been explained to the clients. The various terms used in the agreement were carefully defined in a schedule.

13. Condition 2 of Schedule 1 to the CFA set out the responsibilities of the clients, which were that the clients must –

"(2.1) give FW full, proper and timely instructions that allow FW to work properly;

(2.2) not ask FW to work in an improper or unreasonable way;

(2.3) not deliberately or negligently mislead FW;

(2.4) cooperate fully, properly and in a timely manner with FW when asked;

(2.5) pay the Non-Conditional Fees ... within 14 days of receipt of a request for payment ..."

14. Clause 4.9, and Condition 8 of Schedule 1, set out what would happen if FW ended the agreement before the claims ended. By para 8.2 of the Schedule, FW were entitled to end the agreement "if the Clients reject FW's opinion about making a settlement with the Opponent": in that event, the clients would be liable for the non-conditional fees and disbursements and the conditional fees, and also liable to pay the success fee if they went on to win the claim. By para 8.5:

> "FW can end this agreement if the Clients do not meet their responsibilities in Condition 2. FW is then entitled to decide whether the Clients must
>
> (a) pay FW's Non-Conditional Fees, Conditional Fees and disbursements but not the Success Fee, when FW asks for them; or
>
> (b) pay FW's Non-Conditional Fees, Conditional Fees and disbursements, and the Success Fee if the Clients go on to win the claim."

15. Condition 10 of that Schedule provided amongst other things for FW to have a right to preserve their lien until all monies owed under the CFA had been paid in full.

16. Schedule 2 to the agreement set out the reasons for the level of the success fee. It referred to the advice which counsel had previously given about the prospects of success. It pointed out the defendants denied all liability, and added:

> "This is a complex case which depends substantially on the oral evidence of witnesses and experts. There are also difficult questions of law involved."

17. It is clear from the correspondence that Mr Krishnani was happy, and indeed grateful, to enter into that agreement on behalf of both KMS Ltd and Reachbyte Ltd. At para 38 of his judgment Master Rogers made a finding that the terms of the agreement had been fully explained to Mr Krishnani before he signed it. That important finding is not the subject of any challenge in this appeal.

18. FW had to do a great deal of work to prepare KMS's case for trial. It is their case that Mr Krishnani was a difficult client to deal with, prone to changing his instructions and with a tendency to outbursts of anger. Mr Krishnani accepts a degree of volatility.

However, the working relationship between him (as, in effect, the human embodiment of KMS) and FW continued over a period of nearly a year. FW point out that it was during that period that BD for the first time in the litigation made offers of settlement.

19. It is relevant to note that during that period FW's interim bills (giving details of the work done, the time spent, and the fee earner engaged, and also giving details of disbursements which had been paid or were to be paid) were rendered to KMS and were paid substantially without demur. Four qualifications to that general proposition need to be stated. Firstly, Mr Krishnani did question a letter in September 2006 in which FW pointed out various unexpected developments in the proceedings, and gave an increased estimate of their fees. Secondly, Mr Krishnani again objected to the level of fees in January 2007, though he was simultaneously complaining that some work was being done by junior members of the solicitors' team rather than by senior members (whose hourly rates would of course have been higher). Thirdly, in the course of the BD litigation an order for costs was made against KMS in relation to an application concerning disclosure: Mr Krishnani was angry at the way in which that application had been handled, and for that reason objected to his company being ordered to pay the costs. Fourthly, Mr Krishnani's case is that he often raised oral objections to the amount of the fees which were being incurred, though he did not want to rock the boat too much. Notwithstanding those qualifications, the overall picture is, as I have said, broadly one of payment without demur. Mr Krishnani had requested that interim bills be sent monthly, presumably so that he could keep track of the costs being incurred. The costs were, in the aggregate, very substantial; but that was only to be expected, as the BD litigation was itself substantial and complex, and Mr Krishnani had transferred his instructions from DKLL solicitors to FW precisely because he wanted a bigger firm with greater expertise in the relevant field. It seems to me that the clear inference to be drawn from his payment of those bills is that he was broadly content with the fees which KMS charged.

20. The BD litigation was set down for a five-week hearing of preliminary issues commencing on 2 March 2007. On 21 December 2006 BD made a without prejudice offer to pay £4.2 million in settlement: more than double the first offer they had made. FW wrote to Mr Krishnani explaining KMS's options and advising him to make a counter-offer. They enclosed however an Advice from leading and

junior counsel to the effect that BD's offer was "a very good one and one which clearly ought to be accepted". Mr Krishnani rejected it.

21. Soon after that, KMS ran into difficulties which caused the litigation to end in disaster for them. I set out below a more detailed chronology, but in a nutshell the difficulties related to the relationship between Messrs Krishnani, Craze and Symes, and the ability of Mr Symes to act as a properly independent expert witness.

22. I have indicated above that Messrs Craze and Symes had received payment for their work in the litigation from Mr Krishnani rather than from KMS's solicitors. It was Mr Krishnani's case that he made payments to Mr Craze personally, and expected Mr Craze to pass on to Mr Symes the appropriate sums by way of payment for Mr Symes' work. However, as eventually emerged, the invoices for the work in question did not come from either Mr Craze or Mr Symes. Instead, they came initially (from about November 2003 until mid-2004) from Dawn Traders Ltd, a company set up by Mr Craze and members of his family; and latterly, from July 2004, they came from Square Mile Investment Consultants Ltd ("Square Mile"). Square Mile was incorporated in May 2004: its directors and shareholders were Mr Craze and Mr Symes. Its website described it as assisting investors who had been ill-advised or defrauded by stockbrokers or financial advisers.

23. FW's case has always been that they had no knowledge of Square Mile until the later events to which I will come shortly. In this regard, there was a conflict of evidence about a lunch meeting on 4 July 2006 between Mr Craze and Mr Greager of FW. Mr Craze gave evidence to Master Rogers to the effect that in the course of this lunch he told Mr Greager all about what Square Mile did ("though not, it would appear, Mr Symes' involvement therewith": see para 53 of Master Rogers' judgment). Mr Greager gave evidence that Mr Craze did mention a company, but gave the impression that it was in the process of looking for business and might be able to work with FW in the future. Having seen and heard both witnesses, Master Rogers accepted the evidence of Mr Greager and rejected that of Mr Craze. KMS accept that he was entitled to do so, and there is no appeal against that finding of fact. It is, in my view, a highly significant finding when considering the attack upon other findings made by Master Rogers.

24. The evidence before Master Rogers showed that FW, and

counsel instructed on behalf of KMS, had been concerned for some time about the relationship between Mr Krishnani & Mr Symes.

25. On 7 June 2006 Mr Krishnani had sent to FW a draft expert report prepared by Mr Symes. He had annotated this with suggested additions and deletions. One annotation in particular (about which Mr Krishnani gave very unsatisfactory evidence when cross examined before Master Rogers: see para 58 of the judgment) comprised a suggested revision of the draft preceded by the following parenthesis clearly addressed to Mr Craze: "(Dear Tony I have discussed with you about this please redo on following lines)". FW forwarded this annotated draft by email to counsel, expressing concern that Mr Krishnani "is now saying he is not happy with the report, that he now wants to prepare the report himself with Tony Craze ... and that we should not tell JS about this for the time being. This of course presents many problems but as you know Kris can be quite insistent ...". Leading counsel agreed to speak to Mr Krishnani and explain that the expert report must be the work of Mr Symes alone.

26. There followed on 9 June 2006 a telephone conference in which leading counsel stressed to Mr Krishnani the particular concern of the courts that there should be a distance between an expert witness, the clients and the lawyers; that it was important for Mr Symes to keep that distance; and that Mr Symes could at trial be cross-examined about any closeness to other witnesses and to the lawyers. Mr Krishnani said that he had reservations about Mr Symes' report (his concern apparently being, or including, that Mr Symes did not express himself with sufficient clarity), that he had discussed things with Mr Craze, and that he had asked Mr Craze to comment. Leading counsel specifically advised that it was not appropriate for another expert to rewrite the report. Mr Krishnani did not say anything about Square Mile. Nor did he say anything about the invoices which he was receiving in respect of the work of Messrs Craze and Symes.

27. As the trial against BD approached, there were a number of problems over KMS's disclosure. It was found that some documents had not been disclosed as they should have been, and that a substantial number of original documents which had been in the possession of Mr Krishnani had been destroyed. As FW were grappling with those problems, BLG wrote letters dated 8 February 2007 to FW, and to Mr Symes (with a copy to FW), which called into question Mr Symes' independence as an expert witness, and the relationship between Mr

Symes and Mr Craze. BLG indicated that they had reason to think that Mr Symes' reports were not his independent work; that the reports had been influenced by Mr Craze, who was understood to have a connection with Mr Krishnani; and that Mr Symes may not have the necessary independence to act as an expert witness. Each of these letters demanded prompt and full answers to a series of detailed questions exploring those areas of concern, and prompt disclosure of any relevant documents. In particular, questions were asked as to whether any business or company for which Mr Craze was an agent, employee, director or shareholder had received, or was due to receive, any (and if so, what) payment from Mr Krishnani. Questions were also asked as to Mr Symes' connections with Mr Craze and with Mr Krishnani "whether directly, or indirectly through Mr Craze". Master Rogers was satisfied on the evidence that copies of both letters were sent by FW to Mr Krishnani (see para 60 of the judgment).

28. On 13 February 2007 Mr Krishnani travelled to India, and did not return until February 23. It was understandable that he made that journey, because his brother in law was dangerously ill, but it was an added complication that he was not available in person to discuss matters with his solicitors at a critical time. However, communication by telephone and email was of course perfectly possible save when Mr Krishnani was travelling.

29. On February 15 Mr Craze went to FW's offices to provide his response to the questions posed by BLG. A detailed note was taken by FW. By the following day FW had produced a draft letter embodying Mr Craze's responses: this letter has conveniently been referred to as "the Craze letter", although it was written and sent by FW. Mr Symes, as will be seen, prepared a separate letter of his own in response to the questions which BLG had asked of him: this has been referred to as "the Symes letter".

30. The draft of the Craze letter was sent by FW to Mr Craze. It contained a number of gaps which Mr Craze was asked to complete. In response to some of the specific questions, it said that Mr Craze had only received payments from Mr Krishnani personally and would continue to receive payment personally for any work carried out for Mr Krishnani.

31. The draft was also sent by email to Mr Krishnani on 16 February 2007. FW asked Mr Krishnani to read and comment on it, emphasising that it was important for him to review the information

in the letter because he needed to be comfortable with what was said. His response was short and vigorous: he made one minor correction to a date, and asked for the paragraphs relating to payments, and to the role played by Mr Craze, to be deleted. Mr Krishnani said "It is not their business to know who is helping me and why or any monetary arrangements of Mr Craze". Mr Krishnani did not take this opportunity to tell his solicitors about the manner in which he had been invoiced for, and paid, the fees charged to him by Mr Craze and Mr Symes. On the contrary, he sought to exclude any reference to the topic of financial arrangements. It is submitted on behalf of FW that it is significant to note, and no coincidence, that Mr Craze similarly said nothing about the way in which his and Mr Symes' fees had been invoiced.

32. A revised draft was prepared which did not exclude the paragraphs which Mr Krishnani had wanted to exclude. By email sent at 1926 on 22 February 2007, FW sent this revised draft to Mr Craze, and asked him to provide the information needed to complete certain blanks, including details of payments received. A copy was also emailed to Mr Krishnani, but as I understand it he was by this time travelling from India back to England. Mr Craze provided the requested details, and as a result FW sent the final version of the Craze letter to BLG at 1538 on February 23. Amongst other things it said that the sums paid by Mr Krishnani to Mr Craze, by calendar year, were as follows: nothing in 2003; £22,000 in 2004; £6,500 in 2005; and £28,000 in 2006. It also said, in answer to some of the specific questions which had been posed by BLG:

> "(e) No business/company for which Mr Craze is an agent, employee, director or shareholder has ever received any form of payment from Mr Krishnani.
>
> (f) Mr Craze will continue to receive payments for any work he does for Mr Krishnani on the same basis as set out above.
>
> (g) No business/company for which Mr Craze is an agent, employee, director or shareholder is due to receive any form of payment from Mr Krishnani."

33. At 1556 on 23 February 2007 a copy of that final letter was emailed to Mr Krishnani. He did not volunteer any information to his solicitors about Square Mile or about the invoices from that company.

It is submitted by Mr Hill-Smith that Mr Krishnani regarded himself as having made payments to Mr Craze personally, and so did not regard the terms of the Craze letter as inaccurate. Mr Bacon submits that Mr Krishnani had deliberately withheld that information throughout the drafting of the Craze letter, and had thereby caused his solicitors to send out what was in fact an inaccurate letter.

34. Meanwhile, Mr Symes had completed and sent (on 19 February 2007) his own letter in reply to BLG's enquiries. He described the circumstances in which he had first met Mr Craze many years ago, referred to a time in 2001/2 when Mr Craze had shown interest in a business which Mr Symes was trying to set up, and continued: "After that initial meeting we continued to meet occasionally for a drink at lunch time. Having failed to raise the required capital to launch the business I decided to retire. Mr Craze and I continued to meet on my rare visits to the city for a drink and a chat." It is common ground between the parties that that part of the Symes letter was a serious untruth.

35. In the course of Friday, February 23, FW sent an email to Mr Krishnani advising him of the agenda for a consultation with counsel on the Monday morning. That agenda included the following: "Symes impartiality etc – we need more details on this".

36. Later on February 23, Mrs Mehta made an application to the court seeking to exclude Mr Symes from giving evidence as an expert witness for KMS. She attached to her application copies of the Square Mile website and details of the directors and shareholders of Square Mile.

37. On the Saturday, February 24, Mr Symes reported to FW that he had suffered a haemorrhage and was unwell. He played no further part in the relevant events, and was not called as a witness before Master Rogers.

38. At the consultation which began at 11:00 on Monday February 26 a number of topics were discussed. They included matters relating to Messrs Symes and Craze, and the fact that they were directors of Square Mile. By this stage BLG had made clear that their clients would be joining with Mrs Mehta in seeking to exclude Mr Symes from giving expert evidence at the (now imminent) trial. In cross examination Mr Krishnani ultimately admitted that he had seen and read the Symes letter on February 26. He still did not say anything in

the consultation about his having been invoiced by Square Mile for the work of both Mr Symes and Mr Craze.

39. At 22:39 that night, BLG sent a letter to FW pointing out that Square Mile's website showed that it was a claimants' adviser whose business consisted in pursuing claims like the ones in the litigation. The letter contended that Mr Symes could have no excuse for having failed to disclose that he was a co-director with Mr Craze of a company set up to provide expert witness services for claimants against stockbroking firms, and that Mr Symes' assertions that Mr Craze had had no input into his reports could not be reconciled with documents recently disclosed. BLG asked amongst other things for disclosure of all invoices raised by Mr Symes in relation to his expert witness work in the case. They also asked for a statement as to whether Square Mile had received, directly or indirectly, any fees in relation to Mr Symes' work, and/or in relation to work which Mr Craze had done with Mr Symes, in the BD litigation. Mr Krishnani received a copy of this letter on the following day, February 27. He did not volunteer to FW any information about the Square Mile invoices.

40. Before Master Rogers, Mr Greager gave evidence as to the impact of BLG's letter. He pointed out that BLG were clearly going to allege that Messrs Craze, Symes and Krishnani were "all, as it were, in bed together". The independence of Mr Symes as an expert witness could now be the subject of a formidable attack, and so too – because of the untruthful content of the Symes letter – could his credibility. As Mr Greager summarised the position in relation to Messrs Symes and Craze: "They are joint shareholders, directors and they set up a website and they go round touting for this kind of business. He lied about that so that's the problem."

41. On February 28 FW wrote to Mr Krishnani expressing their astonishment that they had not previously been told by Mr Symes that he and Mr Craze were co-directors of Square Mile. The letter warned Mr Krishnani in blunt terms that there was now a serious risk that some or all of Mr Symes' evidence would be excluded, and said that without expert evidence they did not see how KMS could win the case. The letter concluded by advising Mr Krishnani that KMS should accept BD's earlier offer without further delay, and warning that they would invoke clause 8.2 of the CFA if that advice was not followed.

42. That letter was emailed to Mr Krishnani at 12:38. In a telephone call later that afternoon, Mr Krishnani told FW that Mr

Craze had visited him that morning. He gave the impression that he had been misled about the involvement of Mr Symes in Square Mile, and he still did not volunteer any information about the Square Mile invoices he had received. FW's attendance note of what Mr Krishnani said reads in part as follows: "this morning TC came to office – I said so far as I'm concerned can't see why Symes had to write that letter ... I suggested to TC to come clean and write to BLG ...". I refer below to a particular feature of the evidence which Master Rogers heard about this conversation between Messrs Krishnani and Craze.

43. There were further negotiations between FW and BLG, but these did not bear fruit. BD's earlier offer was withdrawn before Mr Krishnani tried to accept it, and on March 1 BD proposed what has been referred to as a "drop hands" settlement which in broad terms would bring the BD litigation to an end without any damages being paid, and would leave KMS to bear their own costs.

44. In prompt response to a request for invoices made on March 1 by FW, Mr Krishnani sent to FW 28 pages of Dawn Traders and Square Mile invoices and statements. These showed that each of those companies had invoiced Mr Krishnani for the work of both Mr Craze and Mr Symes. These documents showed moreover that each company had acknowledged receipt of payment of their respective invoices. In short, the paperwork showed that Mr Krishnani had paid Dawn Traders, and latterly Square Mile, for all the work which Messrs Craze and Symes had done in relation to the BD litigation.

45. FW regarded those invoices and statements as very damaging to KMS's case. They were right to do so. The expert evidence of Mr Symes was important to KMS's prospects of success; BD and Mrs Mehta were already equipped with strong grounds to challenge his ability to give independent evidence; and the very late revelation of documents showing that his and Mr Craze's work had been invoiced by Dawn Traders and Square Mile, and that those companies had acknowledged receipt of payment, strengthened their position yet further. The documents themselves were very damaging, showing as they did that KMS's expert and Mr Krishnani's adviser were in business together, with obvious consequences for the perception of Mr Symes' independence; and they were made all the worse by their being disclosed so very late in the day. It remains Mr Krishnani's case, despite these documents, that he always regarded himself as paying Mr Craze personally for the work of Mr Symes and Mr Craze. It is

however difficult to understand, if that is the case, why the company documents ever came into existence, and why all three men failed for so long to mention the documents.

46. On March 2, at 12:45, there was a consultation attended by Mr Krishnani, counsel, and the solicitors who had worked on the case (with the exception of Mr Greager, who was fulfilling a long-standing commitment to attend a meeting in Spain). It was a difficult consultation for all concerned. A detailed note was kept by Miss Roake, and a typescript of it was later prepared. KMS accept that it is an accurate record. Leading counsel outlined the problems caused by, amongst other things, the deliberate lie told in the Symes letter, and the Square Mile invoices. He also referred to the problems caused by the destruction of original documents. He summarised the present position as being that things had moved on dramatically for the worse.

47. Mr Krishnani was shown the Symes letter. He said he had not read it until he returned from India. As summarised in the note, Mr Krishnani then went on: "I asked TC and JS why they lied. TC said it was not that bad. I asked TC to come clean. As far as I'm concerned – doesn't make a difference". Leading counsel pointed out to Mr Krishnani that it would be said against him that he knew Mr Symes "was part of the litigation team". The note continues with the following exchange between Mr Krishnani and counsel:

"CDK: I knew they were friends.

[Leading counsel]: You must have known more than that."

48. Leading counsel indicated that there would be an application by the other parties to disqualify Mr Symes from giving evidence. He went on to spell out to Mr Krishnani the limited options available to KMS, and the risks involved in doing anything other than accepting the "drop hands" offer. Mr Krishnani appears to have wavered (understandably, since he faced a very unhappy situation), but eventually indicated that he would accept that offer. Mr Dykins said he needed to speak to Mr Greager before any decision was made, because of implications for the CFA. The meeting was then adjourned for refreshments, and Mr Dykins made a telephone call to Mr Greager in Spain.

49. When the meeting resumed, at about 14:30, it appears that Mr

Krishnani was inclined to fight on. However, Mr Dykins immediately handed to Mr Krishnani a letter in the following terms:

"We hereby give you notice of termination of the CFA dated 29 March 2006, effective immediately. Any further work which we undertake on your and/or the claimants' behalf, including accepting the settlement offer from BD which lapses at 4.00 pm today (if that is what you decide to do), will be charged at our normal rates and according to our normal terms of business. We will let you have an engagement letter confirming these in full."

50. Just over two hours later, at 16:48, Mr Krishnani instructed FW to accept the "drop hands" offer from BD. He indicated that he felt he had no option but to accept that offer once the CFA had been terminated.

51. The importance of the sequence of those last two events is this. FW's case is that having terminated the CFA pursuant to condition 8(5) they were entitled to bill their clients for the full amount of their ordinary fees, which they subsequently did. Had the CFA still been in force when the "drop hands" settlement was concluded, FW would only have been entitled to 70% of their fees, because the proceedings would have ended in failure for their clients. This appeal effectively relates to the 30% difference between those two.

52. Although FW had terminated the CFA their letter had expressed willingness to continue to act on the basis of their ordinary fees being paid, and for a short time they did so. KMS then instructed another firm of solicitors, in particular with reference to the contested assessment in the Sibley litigation. FW held papers relevant to that assessment, and the new solicitors wanted to obtain them.

53. On 22 March 2007 FW wrote to Mr Krishnani referring to their termination of the CFA pursuant to conditions 8.2 and 8.5(a), and asserting their entitlement to payment of both their unconditional and their conditional fees for all work done until 3.15 pm on 2 March 2007. Their letter went on to refer to certain monies which had been received from BLG in connection with the BD litigation, and indicated that those funds would be applied in settlement of their outstanding fees. FW sent with that letter their statement of account, which showed total fees of £1,276,288.53 and a balance outstanding (after taking into account interim invoices paid) of £441,089.89.

54. There was an issue before Master Rogers as to whether Mr

Krishnani had received and read this letter at the time. Master Rogers found that he had. There is no appeal against that finding, which it is accepted Master Rogers was entitled to make. That is hardly surprising, since Mr Krishnani had admitted receipt of the statement of account which had been enclosed with the letter. It is however an important finding in relation to Mr Krishnani's credibility, and it is relevant to note that Master Rogers (at para 76 of his judgment) commented on this part of Mr Krishnani's evidence in the following terms:

> "I am afraid that this is only one of many examples where I was wholly unconvinced by [Mr Krishnani's] evidence."

55. I should note that condition 8.2 was not relied upon in Mr Bacon's submissions to the Master or to me. However, it does not seem to me that anything turns on that. It is true, as Mr Hill-Smith points out, that the letter of 22 March 2007 did not give particulars of the breach of condition 8.5, but it seems to me that Mr Krishnani must have known full well why FW had terminated the CFA.

56. Bills were subsequently sent which related to work done after the termination of the CFA, and work done in relation to the Sibley litigation. These are not relevant to this appeal.

57. On 1 May 2007 FW wrote noting that Mr Krishnani had now instructed new solicitors in connection with the Sibley litigation, and requiring payment of their outstanding bills before they would release the papers to those new solicitors. The total amount then outstanding, in relation to six invoices which had either not been paid or had only been paid in part, was £144,498.63. However:

i) Inv 41138 related to counsel's fees;
ii) Inv 41217 did relate to work done on the BD litigation, but only £2,266.36 was outstanding;
iii) Invs 41594 and 41602 related to work done after the termination of the CFA or in relation to the Sibley litigation;
iv) Inv 41581 was mostly for disbursements, with solicitors' work in relation to the BD litigation amounting to little more than £550;
v) Inv 41883 was for a total of £84,688.60 disbursements. The vast majority of the charges were for photocopying and other expenses of document preparation in connection with the BD litigation. The bill did however also include some charges for taxi fares and meals

when one of the solicitors was working late on the case. These charges amounted to about £400 in total.

58. On 5 May 2007 Mr Krishnani replied referring to his unhappiness over the outcome of the BD litigation and saying:

> "There are certain elements of the account which I want to discuss with you and hopefully reach agreement."

59. That letter went on to refer to the Sibley litigation, indicating that Mr Krishnani would be happy for FW (and leading counsel) to deal with that matter:

> "if we can agree a reasonable fixed amount that I have to pay and then if you want there is an uplift on the success of the claim."

60. In the ensuing exchange of emails, FW indicated that there was no scope for a reduction in the outstanding bills. They also pointed out that if the new solicitors were taking over, they would need time to prepare for the assessment hearing in the Sibley litigation, and that accordingly FW must be paid by 14 May 2007 so that either they could do the necessary work or the papers could be released to the new solicitors for that purpose. On May 10, FW emailed Mr Krishnani again, asking him whether they would be paid by the 14th. By email of May 11 Mr Krishnani replied expressing his disappointment that FW were not willing to compromise. In the course of this letter he said:

> "I am disappointed with the way this matter was dealt with and costs paid to Barlow Lyde on the disclosure application. You have asked for taxi fares/meals etc which I do not think were part of arrangement. Your cost estimate are not accurate ... Under protest I will settle your account and expect the papers to be immediately transferred to [the new solicitors]. I now formally demand that you tax/assess your costs pursuant to Solicitors Act 1974."

61. Payment was then made of the outstanding amount, and the papers were transferred to the new solicitors. They wrote to FW on 1 June 2007, saying amongst other things –

> "As you will recall, Mr Krishnani has settled the balance of your account under protest and asked that you have your fees assessed. He has not heard from you to confirm your intentions, and therefore I presume that

you have elected, as is your right, to decline to accept the invitation and force him to make an application."

62. On 13 August 2007 KMS issued a Part 8 application seeking "an order in standard form pursuant to s 70 of the Solicitors Act 1974 for the detailed assessment of the defendant's bill dated 21.03.07".

63. Section 70 of the 1974 Act, so far as material, provides:

"(1) Where before the expiration of one month from the delivery of a solicitor's bill an application is made by the party chargeable with the bill, the High Court shall, without requiring any sum to be paid into court, order that the bill be taxed and that no action be commenced on the bill until the taxation is completed.

(2) Where no such application is made before the expiration of the period mentioned in subsection (1), then, on an application being made by the solicitor or, subject to subsections (3) and (4), by the party chargeable with the bill, the court may on such terms, if any, as it thinks fit (not being terms as to the costs of the taxation), order –

   (a) that the bill be taxed; and

   (b) that no action be commenced on the bill, and that any action already commenced be stayed, until the taxation is completed.

(3) Where an application under subsection (2) is made by the party chargeable with the bill ...

   (c) after the bill has been paid, but before the expiration of twelve months from the payment of the bill,

   no order shall be made except in special circumstances and, if an order is made, it may contain such terms as regards the costs of the taxation as the court may think fit."

64. It was FW's case that the bill had already been paid in full, and that accordingly KMS would have to show special circumstances justifying an order for detailed assessment. On 10 September 2007 Master Rogers directed a preliminary hearing "to determine whether there are any special circumstances within the meaning of s 70(3)(c) and, if there are, the terms as to costs on which any future assessment may proceed ('the preliminary issue')". He also gave directions as to the filing of evidence, directing that FW's evidence "shall include particularisation

of the basis on which the CFA came to be terminated". Subsequently the preliminary issue was expanded to include the issue of whether FW were entitled to terminate the CFA as they did, and in the event the bulk of the main hearing was taken up with that issue.

65. There were further directions hearings before the main hearing was reached. At one, on 10 November 2008, Master Rogers dismissed an application by KMS for an order that FW "plead their case in relation to the termination of the CFA". He did so because in his view the issues were already clear from the detailed witness statements which had been filed.

66. Although it was not a matter which had been raised at any of those interlocutory hearings, KMS made a last-minute attempt, on the day before the main hearing, to raise an issue as to whether KMS had in fact paid FW's bill in full. Their reason for wanting to raise that issue was that if the bill had not been paid, KMS were entitled to require a detailed assessment and would not need to show special circumstances. Master Rogers rejected that application as coming far too late in the day and introducing a substantial new matter. In their written Grounds of Appeal KMS sought to appeal against that decision. At the outset of his submissions before me, however, Mr Hill-Smith indicated that he would not be pursuing that point, and would proceed on the basis that the bill had indeed been paid. I therefore say no more about this.

67. Having heard evidence from Mr Krishnani, Mr Craze, Mr Lawson, Mr Greager and Miss Roake, Master Rogers decided in favour of FW and refused to order a detailed assessment. It is against that decision that this appeal is brought.

68. I have referred above to some of Master Rogers' specific findings of fact. It is relevant to note at this stage the assessment he made of witnesses from whom he heard:

i) Mr Greager's evidence was clear and consistent (para 24 of the judgment).
ii) Miss Roake's evidence was compelling not only in the modest and composed way in which it was given, but also in its consistency and truthfulness (para 26).
iii) Mr Craze was evasive, and unwilling to accept the consequences of the documents relating to payments. As to what was said at the

lunch on 4 July 2006, Master Rogers rejected Mr Craze's evidence and accepted that of Mr Greager (para 31).

iv) Mr Krishnani was a very unsatisfactory witness, unwilling to accept the evidence of documents or of other witnesses who contradicted him. Where his evidence was contradicted by FW's witnesses, Master Rogers "unhesitatingly" rejected Mr Krishnani's evidence and preferred that of Mr Greager and Miss Roake (para 32).

69. So far as is relevant for the purposes of this appeal, Master Rogers' decisions on the issues before him were as follows:

i) KMS were in breach of condition 2 of the CFA (para 79);
ii) FW were entitled to terminate the CFA pursuant to condition 8.5, and so were entitled to charge both their non-conditional and their conditional fees (para 80);
iii) FW did in fact terminate the CFA on the grounds of a breach of condition 2: "Half way through the 'crisis meeting' [Mr Krishnani] was accused of effectively concealing the facts from his legal team and he accepted the termination without complaint" (para 83);
iv) There was no necessity for FW to give reasonable notice because the termination of the CFA did not determine the retainer between them and KMS (para 85);
v) There were no special circumstances entitling KMS to a detailed assessment (para 96).

70. Pursuant to CPR 52.11(1), the appeal is a review, not a rehearing. It will only succeed if Master Rogers was wrong in his decision. Where an appeal involves a challenge to a finding of fact which depended on the trial judge's view as to the credibility of witnesses, an appellant must show that the finding was plainly wrong: see *Assicurazioni Generali SpA v Arab Insurance Group* [2003] 1 WLR 577 at para 12; see also the note at 52.11.4 in the White Book. The importance of the judge's assessment of evidence after cross examination as a tool for determining the truth of disputes between the parties was rightly emphasised by Peter Smith J at para 27 of his judgment in *Sibley & Co v Reachbyte Ltd & KMS Ltd* [2008] EWHC 2665 (Ch).

71. It will be apparent from what I have said above that Master Rogers' findings, and ultimate decision, were heavily dependent upon the view he had formed of the credibility and reliability of the

witnesses from whom he had heard. In this appeal, I of course have had no opportunity to make any such assessment. This case is in my view one in which it would be appropriate to accord considerable weight to that fact.

72. Mr Hill-Smith argued on a number of different grounds that the Master should have found that special circumstances did exist, and that accordingly he was wrong to refuse a detailed assessment. The grounds can conveniently be subdivided into two categories:

i) It is submitted that Master Rogers should have found that FW were not entitled to terminate the CFA as they did. It is agreed between the parties that if the termination of the CFA was unlawful, KMS are entitled to a detailed assessment.

ii) Even if the termination of the CFA was lawful, it is submitted that Master Rogers ought to have found that a combination of some or all of the following four factors amounted to special circumstances:
  a) The fact that there was an express reservation of the right to tax
  b) The fact that payment of the outstanding balance of £144,498 was only made under protest about the amount of the bill
  c) The fact that Mr Krishnani was under pressure to pay the bill because he needed the release to his new solicitors of the papers relating to the Sibleys assessment
  d) The fact that at least some aspects of the bill were disputed, and there was an issue as to whether a particular interim bill (number 41217) had or had not been paid.

73. The first submission turned on the evidence which Master Rogers heard, and on this appeal the submissions are to the effect that his findings of fact should be overturned. In the second category, the submissions on appeal are, in essence, that Master Rogers failed to give any or sufficient weight to the relevant factors, either individually or collectively; that he misdirected himself in law; and that his exercise of his discretion was accordingly flawed. It is because of those submissions that I have felt it necessary to summarise the history of relevant events in some detail above.

74. I will deal first with the issues relating to the termination of the CFA. Master Rogers found that KMS was in breach of condition 2 of the CFA and that FW was entitled to terminate the CFA. In that regard, he made (amongst others) the following findings as to credibility and as to the facts:

i) The Square Mile invoices made it quite clear that Square Mile had invoiced Mr Krishnani direct for the work done by Mr Symes and Mr Craze. He did not accept the evidence of Mr Craze to the effect that all monies were paid to him personally, and that he in turn paid Mr Symes (para 63 of the judgment).
ii) On the totality of the evidence, he took the view that Mr Symes and Mr Craze were working together on the expert's report and were not therefore independent, and that Mr Krishnani knew this (para 64).
iii) The attendance notes of the consultation on March 2 indicate that Mr Krishnani was aware of Square Mile and its involvement in the case and had deliberately concealed that fact from FW. He did not accept Mr Krishnani's evidence to the contrary (para 67).
iv) After the termination letter had been handed to him, Mr Krishnani agreed to FW continuing to represent him and accepted he would have to pay their full rates for any further work. It was only some weeks later that the retainer between KMS and FW was terminated (para 70).
v) Contrary to his denial, Mr Krishnani did receive and read FW's letter of 22 March 2007, and the enclosed fee note and accompanying documents (para 76).

75. Mr Hill-Smith acknowledged the difficulties faced by an appellant who seeks to overturn findings of fact. He nonetheless submitted that Master Rogers' findings could not stand, being (as he contended) neither founded on the evidence nor sufficiently supported by any logical analysis.

76. I do not propose (because I do not think it necessary) to deal with the minutiae of each and every one of Mr Hill-Smith's lengthy and detailed submissions. I have considered them all with care, and I have had regard not only to their individual strengths but also to their collective effect.

77. Before considering specific points, it seems to me that it is appropriate to begin with a brief overview. The BD litigation ended disastrously for KMS. It did so because, against a background of problems relating to disclosure, an apparently good case was fatally undermined by the very late revelation of material which gave the opposing parties a good prospect of excluding the expert evidence which KMS needed if it was to win the case. Because of the CFA, that

undermining of the prospects of success had consequences not only for KMS but also for FW. FW had sought to protect themselves against such problems by imposing on KMS the obligation not to mislead them, whether deliberately or negligently. Why, despite that protection, did FW only learn so close to the trial that Mr Symes' independence was open to cogent challenge? Master Rogers found that it was because Mr Krishnani had deliberately misled them.

78. The principal grounds on which his judgment is attacked, as I see it, are the following.

79. Firstly, complaint is made that neither FW nor Master Rogers ever formulated with sufficient precision the allegation of deliberate misleading. The case was, in Mr Hill-Smith's oft-reiterated criticism, beset by the absence of pleadings. He submitted that FW were in effect alleging dishonesty on the part of Mr Krishnani, and such an allegation must be precisely formulated and clearly proved. He further submitted that there is a distinction to be drawn between concealing and misleading, and that Master Rogers relied on evidence of the former as an improper foundation for a finding of the latter.

80. I accept the premise of these submissions – namely, that in the circumstances of this case it was necessary to be clear and precise about what was alleged and proved against Mr Krishnani.

81. However, I reject the submission that Mr Krishnani did not know what he was accused of having done wrong, or that Master Rogers' judgment leaves any doubt as to what finding he made against Mr Krishnani. He said in terms (at para 67) that the attendance notes of the consultation on 2 March 2007 "indicate that [Mr Krishnani] was aware of Square Mile and its involvement in the case and had deliberately concealed that fact from [FW]". He did not accept Mr Krishnani's evidence to the contrary. It is submitted by Mr Hill-Smith that in that paragraph Master Rogers was mistakenly proceeding on the basis that Mr Krishnani had made an admission of knowledge and concealment at the consultation on 2 March 2007. I agree that the detailed note of that consultation does not contain anything which could properly be regarded as such an admission, and, with respect to Master Rogers, I accept that this paragraph in the judgment might have been more felicitously expressed. I do not however accept the submission that Master Rogers fell into error. In my view, the sentence in para 67 beginning "These documents indicate ..." is a statement of Master Rogers' inference from the evidence as to what was said by Mr

Krishnani and by leading counsel at that consultation. It is apparent from the attendance note that Mr Krishnani had no convincing answer to leading counsel's observation (quoted in para 47 above) "You must have known more than that". My view is strengthened by para 83 of the judgment, in which Master Rogers summarised what happened on March 2 as being that Mr Krishnani "was accused of effectively concealing the facts from his legal team and he accepted the termination without complaint".

82. I also reject the submission that in the circumstances of this case there is any significance in the distinction Mr Hill-Smith draws between concealing and misleading. In order to decide whether to take the risk as to their costs which the CFA involved, FW had to make an assessment of the prospects of success in the BD litigation. They needed from Mr Krishnani a complete and honest account of all relevant matters, and they imposed an obligation on their clients not to mislead them. Mr Krishnani, as the Master found, knew of Square Mile and of its involvement in the case. He knew, from at latest his telephone discussion with leading counsel on 9 June 2006, the importance of Mr Symes being, and being seen to be, independent. Yet he failed to tell his solicitors what he knew, even when it was obvious that BLG were pressing hard for all relevant information as to the payment of Messrs Craze and Symes. As Mr Bacon submitted, the obvious inference is that he knew how badly his case would be damaged by the link between Messrs Craze and Symes. Master Rogers was in my judgment entitled to find that such failure amounted to a deliberate misleading.

83. Secondly, Mr Hill-Smith points to the evidence of both Mr Krishnani and Mr Craze to the effect that, despite the appearance to the contrary of the Dawn Traders and Square Mile invoices, all payments had in fact been made by Mr Krishnani to Mr Craze personally, and had been passed on as appropriate by Mr Craze to Mr Symes personally. He submits that there was no or no sufficient basis for Master Rogers' rejection of that evidence. It is said that the evidence was not even challenged in cross-examination. Reliance is placed on the fact that there were produced, in the course of the hearing, statements of a bank account in the name of Square Mile which did not show any receipt of monies from Mr Krishnani. These related to an HSBC account in the name of Square Mile, and showed that throughout the relevant period that account had a modest balance

and almost no activity. Mr Hill-Smith submits that there was no basis on which Master Rogers could prefer the inference from the Square Mile invoices and statements to the direct testimony of the two witnesses. He cites para 157 of the decision of the Court of Appeal in *Conlon v Simms* [2008] 1 WLR 484 in support of the principle, which I readily accept, that "a finding that a witness is unreliable does not in itself justify a finding of fact which is directly contrary to his evidence in the absence of other evidence before the court sufficient to justify that finding".

84. Although I accept that principle, I reject Mr Hill-Smith's submissions in this regard as plainly wrong. Master Rogers did not only have the evidence of Mr Krishnani and Mr Craze, and he was not obliged to accept what they said. Their oral testimony was contradicted by the documents. He was in my judgment entitled to conclude from the evidence as a whole that the invoices showed the correct position. The totality of the evidence included the following features, to which in my view Mr Hill-Smith's submissions failed to accord appropriate weight:

i) The absence of any satisfactory explanation from either witness as to why the invoices and statements of account were in the form they were if the true position was as the witnesses claimed.

ii) The fact that Mr Krishnani had never mentioned the role of Square Mile and Dawn Traders until specifically asked to produce invoices, even though BLG were clearly pressing for full disclosure of anything relating to the payment of Messrs Craze and Symes, and had on the contrary sought – when such questions were first raised by BLG – to avoid any reference at all to the financial arrangements between himself and Mr Craze.

iii) The fact that neither Mr Craze nor Mr Symes had ever mentioned the roles of the two companies either, and that Mr Symes had told a direct lie about the nature and extent of his working relationship with Mr Craze. Mr Craze admitted in cross examination that on the face of the documents, it did look as if the money was going to the companies, though he maintained it had in fact gone to the individuals. As I have already observed, one is bound to wonder why it is, if the involvement of those companies was really believed to be insignificant, that all three gentlemen kept quiet about it for so long.

iv) Mr Krishnani's experience and considerable success as a businessman, and the consequent implausibility of any suggestion that he paid no attention to the names on the invoices, and/or did not think it mattered whether or not his expert witness and his "case manager" were directors of the company which invoiced for, and acknowledged receipt of, the fees for their respective services.
v) The fact that Mr Craze was declaring to Companies House that Square Mile was non-trading when the company was issuing the invoices and acknowledging receipt of payment.

85. In my judgment, Master Rogers was entitled to draw the inference from those features that Mr Krishnani knew the significance of the invoices, knew the likely adverse effect on the prospects of success in the litigation if they came to light, and so had kept them from his solicitors until he was unable to conceal them any longer. He was entitled to reject as wholly implausible Mr Krishnani's reiterated claims that he took no interest in the invoicing arrangements and simply regarded himself as paying Mr Craze personally.

86. I should refer at this point to an application made to me by KMS in the course of the appeal. It was not possible to complete all submissions in the time available for the hearing, and it was accordingly necessary to adjourn for a few days with the appeal part-heard. KMS took advantage of that break in proceedings to serve an application to introduce fresh evidence in the form of an affidavit by Mr Krishnani, to which were exhibited copies of paid cheques. KMS wished to rely on these as confirming that cheques made personally to either Mr Craze or Mr Symes, and tallying with the payments recorded as having been received by Dawn Traders and Square Mile, had been paid by Mr Krishnani from a number of different accounts. Objection was taken to this application, and Mr Hill-Smith very sensibly submitted that it would be convenient for me to take note of the evidence, continue with the hearing, and adjudicate upon the application in this judgment.

87. By CPR 52.11(2), "Unless it orders otherwise, the appeal court shall not receive ... (b) evidence which was not before the lower court". The helpful notes at 52.11.2 in the White Book confirm that the *Ladd* v *Marshall* [1954] 1 WLR 1489 criteria for admitting fresh evidence remain relevant in this regard. In my judgment, this proposed fresh evidence fails at least two of those criteria:

i) It is plainly evidence which could with reasonable diligence have been obtained for use before Master Rogers. Even if there was a difficulty about ready access to paid cheques, other sources (such as personal bank account statements) could have provided similar information. I reject the submission that KMS could not have been expected to foresee that there would be any issue about it: given the obvious importance of the overall issue as to the Square Mile invoices, one would have expected KMS to *want* to put forward all relevant evidence from the outset.

ii) In any event, I do not regard the proposed evidence as being such as would probably have an important influence on the result of the case. It raises more questions than it answers. The figures do not tally with the figures given in the final version of the Craze letter for the sums paid year by year to Mr Craze. It is surprising that four different bank accounts were used to make the payments. Moreover, the proposed new material can do nothing to assist KMS on the questions of why the Dawn Traders and Square Mile invoices and statements of account ever came into existence if they do not reflect the reality of the situation, and why Mr Krishnani never mentioned them.

88. I therefore decline to receive this fresh evidence, and return to consideration of the grounds on which KMS attack Master Rogers' judgment.

89. Thirdly, it is said that Master Rogers in his judgment made a number of factual errors and omissions which undermine the validity of his conclusions. In particular, it is submitted that he made a serious error in para 64 of his judgment, when he said that Mr Craze had given evidence that "after these invoices came to light [Mr Krishnani] had asked him (Mr Craze) if he would replace them with invoices from Mr Craze personally to [Mr Krishnani] (or his companies)". FW agree with KMS that the evidence before the Master was in fact to the opposite effect: that it was Mr Craze who had offered to arrange for replacement invoices for his own and Mr Symes' work, and that Mr Krishnani had rejected the offer. KMS submit that the error was a very important one, because Master Rogers said of the evidence which he wrongly attributed to Mr Craze

"... it supports the view which I held having heard the totality of the evidence that Mr Symes/Mr Craze were working together on the experts report and were not therefore independent and, crucially, that [Mr Krishnani] knew this."

90. It is agreed between the parties that Master Rogers' summary of this part of the evidence was factually incorrect, and it follows that his finding on this specific point could not be sustained. I have considered carefully whether it was an error of such significance that it undermines his overall findings of fact and conclusions. In my judgment, it does not. The fact which he mistakenly found was at most a *further* reason for his overall findings and conclusions. As Mr Bacon put it, it was the fact of this discussion which mattered, not who instigated it. The important feature of the meeting between Mr Craze and Mr Krishnani on the morning of 28 February 2007 was that one of them was suggesting the retrospective issue of different invoices, a proposal which raises immediate questions as to how such a thing could even be contemplated, and why anyone would think it could be proper. Mr Hill-Smith makes the fair point that on the evidence in fact given, Mr Krishnani rejected the proposal, and reported to his solicitors the fact that Mr Craze had been to see him. He submits accordingly that the evidence in fact supports Mr Krishnani, yet was wrongly viewed by Master Rogers as something which impugned Mr Krishnani's honesty. That however leaves unanswered the obvious question as to why company invoices had ever been issued in the first place if they did not reflect the reality of the situation. It also leaves unanswered the equally obvious question as to why Mr Krishnani had never said anything about those invoices until specifically asked to produce them.

91. It is relevant in this regard to note a passage from one of Miss Roake's statements, on which Mr Hill-Smith himself sought to rely. At para 75 of her statement of 1 September 2008, Miss Roake said:

"Mr Krishnani may have been making out cheques to John Symes or Tony Craze personally, but that does not alter the fact that he was being invoiced by the company (which was, albeit indirectly, receiving payment)."

92. It seems to me that in that passage Miss Roake was rightly emphasising the importance of the fact that Messrs Craze and Symes were jointly involved in a company which was invoicing Mr Krishnani for the work of both men, and was acknowledging receipt of

payments. That was a key feature of the attack on Mr Symes' ability to give evidence as an independent expert, as was Mr Krishnani's knowledge of their involvement in or connection with Square Mile. Master Rogers was entitled on the evidence as a whole to make his finding that Mr Krishnani deliberately concealed that knowledge from his solicitors, and in my judgment that entitlement is not undermined by the factual error he made in para 64.

93. Mr Hill-Smith helpfully provided a note of the other factual and evidential inaccuracies which he submits are to be found in the judgment. I do not think it necessary to consider these individually. None is as significant as the error in para 64 to which I have referred above, and all are to my mind convincingly answered by Mr Bacon's submissions in reply. In my judgment they do not, either individually or collectively, undermine Master Rogers' overall decision.

94. Fourthly, it is said that Master Rogers did not in his judgment ask himself the right questions, make any sufficiently precise finding of deliberate misleading, make any relevant finding about the Craze letter, or give a sufficient reasoned basis for his findings. Mr Hill-Smith relies on *English v Emery Reimbold & Strick Ltd* [2002] 1 WLR 2409. It is relevant to quote from para 19 of the judgment of the Master of the Rolls in that case:

> "... the judgment must enable the appellate court to understand why the judge reached his decision. This does not mean that every factor which weighed with the judge in his appraisal of the evidence has to be identified and explained. But the issues the resolution of which were vital to the judge's conclusion should be identified and the manner in which he resolved them explained. It is not possible to provide a template for this process. It need not involve a lengthy judgment. It does require the judge to identify and record those matters which were critical to his decision. If the critical issue was one of fact, it may be enough to say that one witness was preferred to another because the one manifestly had a clearer recollection of the material facts or the other gave answers which demonstrated that his recollection could not be relied upon."

95. Relying also on para 6.4 of the judgment of Henry LJ in *Heffer & Knight v Tiffin Green* QBENF 97/1050/1, Mr Hill-Smith submits that this is one of the rare cases in which it can be said that the judgment was:

"... arrived at without sufficient regard being paid to the building blocks of the reasoned judicial process, where the evidence on each issue is marshalled, the weight of the evidence analysed, all tested against the probabilities based on the evidence as a whole, with clear findings of fact and all reasons given."

96. Again, I reject this submission. No doubt it would be possible to rewrite Master Rogers' judgment, expanding upon its contents and amplifying some passages. But with respect to Mr Hill-Smith, it is simply unrealistic to suggest that the reader of Master Rogers' judgment is left uncertain as to why he came to the conclusions he did. It is to my mind entirely plain that he disbelieved key parts of the evidence of Mr Krishnani and of Mr Craze, and concluded from the totality of the evidence that Mr Krishnani had deliberately concealed from his solicitors information which he knew was important. As Henry LJ said in his judgment in *Flannery* v *Halifax Estate Agents* Ltd [2000] 1 WLR 377 at p. 382A (a passage on which Mr Bacon relies), "Where there is a straightforward factual dispute whose resolution depends simply on which witness is telling the truth about events which he claims to recall, it is likely to be enough for the judge (having, no doubt, summarised the evidence) to indicate simply that he believes X rather than Y; indeed, there may be nothing else to say." I cannot see how it would have assisted KMS for Master Rogers to have spelled out in any more detail, or with any greater emphasis, his adverse views of key parts of the evidence of the witnesses called before him on KMS's behalf.

97. For those reasons, I conclude that Master Rogers' finding of breach of condition 2 of the CFA is not open to successful criticism. There is no justification for overturning his findings of fact.

98. So far as the consequences of that breach are concerned, Mr Hill-Smith raised two issues.

99. Firstly, he submits that FW in fact treated Mr Krishnani's conduct as a repudiatory breach of contract, and terminated the CFA on that ground rather than pursuant to condition 8.5. It is true that in his telephone call from Spain during the interlude in the consultation of 2 March 2007 Mr Greager, who did not have the CFA before him, referred to repudiatory breach. Master Rogers was however entitled on the totality of the evidence (including in particular the letter of 22 March 2007) to find, as he did in para 83 of his judgment, that the

CFA was terminated for breach of condition 2. I agree with Master Rogers that the authorities relied on by Mr Bacon – *Laing Management Ltd v Aegon Insurance Co (UK) Ltd* (1997) 86 BLR at p. 76F, and *Dalkia Utilities Services plc v Celtech International Ltd* [2006] EWHC 63 (Comm) at para 143 – support the conclusion on the facts of this case that Mr Krishnani's conduct gave rise both to a contractual right to terminate and to a common law entitlement to accept a repudiatory breach, and that FW were entitled to rely on the former whilst also leaving open a claim for the latter. Mr Greager's initial reference to repudiatory breach is therefore not a reason for rejecting Master Rogers' conclusion.

100. Secondly, Mr Hill-Smith submits that FW were not entitled to terminate the CFA without giving reasonable notice, and that no notice at all was in fact given. He relies in this regard on *Underwood & Piper v Lewis* [1894] QB 306 for the principle that the contract between a solicitor engaged to act in litigation, and his client, is an entire contract which can only be terminated on good cause, and that even then reasonable notice must be given. He also relies on the Law Society's Guide to the Professional Conduct of Solicitors, para 12.12 of which says "A solicitor must not terminate his or her retainer with the client except for good reason and upon reasonable notice". I note that the Guide goes on to give examples of what may be good reasons for termination, which include where there has been "a serious breakdown of confidence between solicitor and client".

101. The CFA itself is silent as to whether any notice is required before FW could exercise their right of termination under condition 8(5). I am not persuaded by Mr Hill-Smith's submission that a requirement of reasonable notice is necessarily to be implied: to take the hypothetical example which I suggested to him in the course of his address, that would leave a solicitor in an impossible position if, at the very door of the court, a client admitted that he had concealed information which greatly reduced his prospects of success in the long and expensive trial which was about to begin. In any event, the answer to this point is in my judgment the answer which Master Rogers gave at para 85: there was no necessity to give reasonable notice of termination of the funding arrangement under the CFA, because the retainer to conduct the litigation continued (and was, indeed, only terminated – by agreement – some weeks later). KMS were not abandoned without representation at a late stage of the litigation: all

that changed was that FW were no longer prepared to accept the risk as to their own costs which they had taken having assessed the prospects of success on the basis of what was now revealed to have been deliberate misleading by Mr Krishnani.

102. For all those reasons I conclude that Master Rogers' finding of breach of condition 2 of the CFA, and his findings as to the consequences of that breach, withstand the prolonged challenge which Mr Hill-Smith has made upon them.

103. I turn to the matters which are relied on as being special circumstances justifying a detailed assessment even if the CFA was lawfully terminated. I will of necessity deal with them individually, but it is of course necessary also to have regard to their combined effect.

104. Mr Hill-Smith submits that there was here an express reservation by KMS of the right to taxation, and that on authority that reservation is a powerful factor in support of a finding of special circumstances. Both parts of that submission are contested by Mr Bacon.

105. Mr Bacon submits that Mr Krishnani's email of 11 May 2007 did not in fact reserve KMS's right to a taxation: rather, it called upon FW to exercise *their* right to seek a taxation. I see the force of that submission, but bearing in mind that the letter was not written by a lawyer I would be reluctant to decide the point against KMS on that basis. It seems to me that the letter might fairly be regarded as a reservation of KMS's rights, albeit clumsily expressed. Accordingly, without making any final decision on that point, I make an assumption in KMS's favour and proceed to consider the other issues as if there had in fact been such a reservation.

106. There is indeed authority to support Mr Hill-Smith's submission as to the importance of such a reservation. In *In re Solicitors* (1934) Times LR 327, Farwell J clearly regarded a reservation of the right to tax as a powerful factor, though he did not say that mere reservation would always be sufficient to amount to special circumstances. In that case, Farwell J found special circumstances where there was a combination of pressure, payment under protest and a reservation. In *Sanders v Isaacs* [1971] 1 WLR 240 Goff J also said that payment with a reservation as to taxation was a highly important factor to be weighed with others. In that case, the reservation was combined with evidence pointing to substantial overcharge, and the exercise of a lien, and Goff J found special

circumstances. Mr Hill-Smith particularly points out that with reference to the principles stated in *Re Boycott* (1885) 29 Ch D 571, and *Re Norman* (1886) 16 QBD 673 – cases on which Mr Bacon relies – Goff J observed (at p. 245C) that "it seems to me that very different considerations apply in the exercise of my undoubted discretion when I come to consider a case where there is such a reservation". Relying on those authorities, Mr Hill-Smith submits that a reservation of a right to tax can be a sufficient special circumstance even in the absence of other factors such as pressure or overcharging: indeed, his submissions were really to the effect that a reservation would often be decisive. He submits that Master Rogers erred in law, and failed to give sufficient weight to the reservation of the right to tax.

107. However, it is important to bear in mind that in a situation such as this the court is being asked to exercise a discretion which only arises if special circumstances are shown, and it is therefore necessary to have regard to all the circumstances of the particular case. I accept that a reservation of the right to tax is a highly important factor, but it is not to be viewed in isolation. The features of the case which I think relevant here are the following:

i) The costs relate to a substantial commercial action, and Mr Krishnani is an experienced, shrewd and successful businessman. In that regard, the nature of the underlying litigation is about as far removed as it could be from that in *In re Solicitors*.

ii) Mr Krishnani had received, and paid without demur, a series of monthly bills in substantial sums. Each bill had been accompanied by a detailed breakdown of the hours claimed, the fee earners involved, and the nature of the work done and disbursements paid. There had been ample opportunity, as the case had gone on, for specific items to be disputed.

iii) The final bill, which prompted Mr Krishnani's letter, did not all relate to the work under the CFA with which this appeal is concerned. Insofar as it did, the bulk of it was for counsel's fees.

iv) Although objection was made, it was in the vaguest of terms. The only items specified were taxi fares and meals. When the bill is examined, these relate to refreshments and transport home for persons who had worked late on the case in FW's offices. They amounted to a very modest sum in the context of the case as a whole, and were similar to other such items which had been paid without demur at earlier stages. There is to my mind great force in Mr Bacon's submission that a query over some taxi fares does not justify detailed assessment of a total bill of more than £1 million.

v) The issue between the parties in reality relates to the 30% difference between the ordinary fees and the non-conditional fees. It is not an issue as to the details of the fees claimed. The hourly rates were agreed long ago, and there has been little if any challenge to the need for FW to undertake all the work for which they claimed payment.

vi) There has never been any evidence to support an allegation that the fees were excessive.

vii) No right to taxation was claimed until after Mr Krishnani had failed in his attempt to persuade FW to agree favourable terms as to their costs of continuing to act in the Sibley litigation.

108. Mr Bacon submits that a modern case such as *Winchester Commodities Group Ltd v RD Black & Co* (HC 1999 00894) provides a more helpful comparison to the facts of this case than do the older authorities relied on by Mr Hill-Smith.

109. I agree with Mr Bacon's submissions to the effect that in a case such as this it would be surprising if relatively minor queries about aspects of a solicitor's bill, raised late in the day and in a manner suggestive of a last attempt to avoid having to pay a bill which was properly charged, could amount to special circumstances. Even if I make the assumption which I have indicated above in favour of KMS, I conclude that in all the circumstance of this case the reservation of the right to tax carries far less weight than it would do in many other cases. I agree with Master Rogers' conclusion, in para 96 of his judgment, that Mr Krishnani's reservation is not here sufficient to amount to a special circumstance justifying detailed assessment of the entire bill.

110. Similar considerations apply in my view to the submissions based on the protest made by Mr Krishnani, and I reach a similar conclusion.

111. It is unfortunate that Master Rogers did not deal specifically with the submission made as to pressure. However, the evidence before him on this point was all one way. KMS knew that the date of the assessment in the Sibley litigation was getting ever closer. They knew they needed to be represented, and that they would have to pay FW's

outstanding bills for the BD litigation before FW would either act in the Sibley litigation or pass the papers to another firm. FW could not be blamed if KMS allowed matters to continue over a period of weeks and thus came under some pressure of time because of the approach of the Sibley hearing. Far from putting KMS under pressure by stressing the need for prompt payment, it seems to me that FW were doing what they were obliged to do. They would surely have been criticised by Mr Krishnani if they had simply let the matter drift until it was too late for them or anybody else to prepare properly for the assessment hearing in the Sibley litigation.

112. The final point made on KMS's behalf relates to minor matters which do not seem to me to provide any support for the appeal. Questions such as whether or not a particular interim payment had been made would arise, and be resolved, whether or not there were a detailed assessment. They do not begin to provide a special circumstance requiring such a detailed assessment. Nor do they add anything to the other matters relied on.

113. In my judgment, Master Rogers – who, it should be remembered, is greatly experienced in these matters – was entitled to conclude that, even taken together, the matters relied upon by KMS were insufficient to make out a case for special circumstances. He made, in my view, no mistake of law or analysis. Nor did he go outside the generous ambit of his discretion. His exercise of his discretion cannot successfully be challenged.

114. For those reasons, this appeal must be dismissed.

115. The parties have provided me with their respective costs schedules, and have helpfully made written submissions as to matters of challenge. I understand it to be accepted by both that having made my decision as to the outcome of the appeal I would proceed to award costs as appropriate, and to make a summary assessment of them with the welcome assistance and expertise of my assessors. It seems to me that in this case there is no reason to depart from the general rule as to costs in CPR 44.3(2)(a) – namely, that the unsuccessful party will be ordered to pay the costs of the successful party. I therefore order KMS to pay FW's costs.

116. It is submitted on behalf of KMS that the claim for costs in relation to the work of Mr Custance of FW should be disallowed, on the basis that he was effectively the client and acting in that capacity. On the authority of *London Scottish Benefit Society v Chorley* (1883)

16 QBD 872, FW are entitled to recover for some of Mr Custance's time, but the time claimed (totalling 18 hours) is unreasonable having regard to the involvement of other solicitors. The costs of his work should be limited to three hours (half an hour on documents, two and a half hours attending at the start and end of the hearing in case he was needed to consider any discussions as to settlement). In relation to Miss Roake, the time spent on documents in Part 2 of the schedule is excessive, and should be reduced to two hours. The hourly rates claimed for the trainee solicitors who worked on the case are too high, and should be reduced to £136 per hour in each case.

117. Making the necessary arithmetical adjustments which flow from the above, the costs of this appeal which KMS must pay to FW are summarily assessed in the total sum of £38,817.60.

Alexander Hill-Smith (instructed by Key2Law) appeared for the claimant/appellant.

Nicholas Bacon (instructed by Fox Williams LLP) appeared for the defendant/respondent.

Editorial Note: The following are decisions of costs judges on criminal cases and therefore do not have the same authority as those at higher judicial level. However, they are included because it is thought they will be of use to the profession.

Case 67
R
v
Gray (Richard)

[2009] 6 Costs LR 967

Supreme Court Costs Office
28 November 2007

Before:
J Simons, Costs Judge

Headnote

The appellant was second junior in a case for only one month before trial, and was awarded by the Determining Officer two-thirds of the "notional" basic fee that would have been paid to his leader. The costs judge rejected this method of calculating a junior's fee, but, on the facts, awarded the appellant only half his leader's actual basic fee.

Reasons for Decision

1. Andrew Smith of counsel appeals in respect of the determination of his brief fee by the Determining Officer at the National Taxing Team

Manchester Region. Mr Smith also appeals in respect of a refresher fee and four conference fees.

2. Mr Smith was appointed as second junior counsel in the defence or Richard Gray who had been charged with others with conspiracy to supply class A drugs. The original Representation Order dated 1 October 2005 permitted representation by solicitor and junior counsel. On 8 March 2006 just under one month from the date of trial on 6 April 2006 the Representation Order was extended to include two junior counsel and accordingly Mr Smith's involvement was for a period of just under one month.

3. The case against all of the defendants was that they took their respective parts in conspiring together with others between 17 July 2005 and 30 September 2005 in supplying cocaine. Gray was alleged by the Crown to be one of the main protagonists in the enterprise. The police had applied for and were granted authority to introduce covert listening devices into commercial premises at unit 9 Penketh Business Park Warrington. In consequence, a substantial amount of covert listening tapes was provided by the prosecution and as much of this material was provided at a very late stage, this was the reason why the representation order was extended to provide representation by two counsel. In addition to the audio material the Crown provided a number of videos which were a condensed version of a more protracted photographic observation.

4. It was Mr Smith's role to go through this material with leading counsel and as a result of his work it became clear to counsel that the major conspiracy that was being alleged by the Crown was nothing of the sort. The defendant wanted a trial and legal argument was prepared. Various admissions were drafted and when these submissions were placed before the Crown it was clear that the prosecution could not sustain the length and breadth of the conspiracy that it had initially alleged.

5. Gray eventually decided to plead guilty and received a sentence of three years. Counsel suggests that had the prosecution succeeded in its original form the defendant was facing imprisonment of between 10 and 15 years.

6. Following the conclusion of the trial leading junior counsel submitted a claim for £66,000. The Determining Officer determined the claim at £30,000 but following a redetermination increased leading junior's fee to £45,000.

7. Mr Smith claimed two thirds of his Leader's fee but was allowed £13,333 which appears to be less than one third of his Leader's fee.

8. In his written reasons the Determining Officer states that he first of all dealt with leading junior's brief fee. In determining Mr Smith's fee the Determining Officer stated that it should be borne in mind that during the greater part of the preparation for trial Mr Smith was not involved. It was not until 8 March 2006 just under a month before the trial that the representation was extended to include two counsel. The Determining Officer then stated:

> "By convention Mr Smith was allowed two thirds of a notionally brief fee for the same period (less than a month) based on his Leader's notionally brief fee for that same period."

9. The Determining Officer in his reasons has gone on to state that he had previously explained this decision to counsel on a number of occasions in that in his view Mr Smith was claiming two thirds of leading junior's brief fee which would have covered a time when leading junior was acting alone. As Mr Smith had requested two thirds of leading junior's fee the appropriate way to allow two thirds was by calculating it on a basis of a notional brief fee for the period of time when there was two counsel.

10. Mr Smith, in his Notice of Appeal, states that at the redetermination the Determining Officer accepted that the case against Gray was the most complex and would attract a higher brief fee than other counsel. He had confirmed that he would increase leading junior's fee accordingly and he accepted that Mr Smith was entitled to two thirds of leading junior's brief fee. Mr Smith states that at no time during the redetermination or at a further meeting with his clerk did the Determining Officer seek to explain any concept of "notional" brief fee. Such a concept had not formed part of the original review hearing and came as a complete surprise to Mr Smith.

11. Mr Smith states that the Determining Officer appears to have accepted the amount of preparation work that had to be done. Mr Smith still had to prepare his case for trial albeit that time was short and consequently the concept of "notional" brief fee fails to recognise the expectation on counsel to be trial ready in whatever time is allowed. Mr Smith's involvement occurred as a result of the Crown's failure to disclose a significant amount of material and it was recognised by the court in order to maintain the trial date that a great

deal of preparation needed to have been completed. That makes it less significant that the leading junior had held the brief fee for a significantly longer time.

12. Mr Smith also states that the Determining Officer in his reasons has not detailed where "the convention" to which he refers can be found or upon which it is based.

13. Mr Smith attended before me at the hearing of this appeal. He informed me that at an oral hearing the Determining Officer informed him that Mr Smith would receive two thirds of his Leader's basic fee but when he received the written reasons it appears that the Determining Officer had only agreed to pay two thirds of a notional fee. Mr Smith submitted that he was not aware of such a concept of notional brief fees and that the fee allowed to him was unreasonable.

14. Whilst he accepted that he only acted for a period of approximately one month nevertheless the time involved was intensive. He estimated that the time spent by him was between 150 to 175 hours. He informed me that he represented a difficult client and that the effect of the work carried out by him contributed to Mr Gray receiving a much lower sentence than could have been expected.

15. Mr Smith's main complaint is with regard to the Determining Officer's decision to allow him a "notional" brief fee. I agree with those submissions. I am unaware of the convention to which the Determining Officer refers with regard to junior counsel when instructed late should only receive two thirds of his Leader's "notional basic fee for the period". In any event, I do not consider it to be an appropriate way to assess junior counsel's fees for a number of reasons the most obvious of which is the difficulty of actually assessing the Leader's fee for a specified period within the whole of the time the Leader is instructed. Assessing a Leader's fee should never be a mathematical exercise. The convention of which I am aware is that a junior should receive one half of his Leader's fee and in special circumstances that should be increased to two thirds of his Leader's fee. In this case whilst I accept that the work carried out by Mr Smith was detailed and intensive I do not consider that it justifies a fee of two thirds of his Leader's fee. Usually two thirds of a Leader's fee is allowed where counsel has had a lengthy involvement in a case both before and at trial. The short period of time in which counsel was involved cannot be ignored. I therefore consider that counsel should receive one half of his Leader's brief fee. His Leader was allowed

£45,000 and accordingly I allow Mr Smith's appeal to the extent that his basic fee should be increased to £22,500.

16. Mr Smith also appeals in respect of the failure of the Determining Officer to provide written reasons for his decisions to disallow a refresher fee and to reduce the fees claimed in respect of four conferences. In his letter to the Determining Officer of 14 May 2007 Mr Smith wrote:

> "I am writing to request that written reasons be given as to the fees allowed to me upon determination and redetermination for the above matter."

17. This request was acknowledged by the National Taxing Team on 16 May 2007 and the written reasons were provided on 6 June 2007. The written reasons have only dealt with Mr Smith's basic fee and the Determining Officer has not provided written reasons in respect of other decisions made by him.

18. Accordingly I direct that the Determining Officer now provides Mr Smith with written reasons for the disallowance of Mr Smith's refresher fee and his reduction of four conferences.

Case 68
R
v
Comer

[2009] 6 Costs LR 972

Supreme Court Costs Office
7 April 2009

Before:
Andrew Gordon-Saker, Costs Judge

Headnote

In this important case, the costs judge had to construe para 24 of Schedule 1 of the 2007 Funding Order (relating to payments to advocates appearing at a court more than 40 kilometres from their office or chambers), and contrasts that wording with the equivalent contained in the earlier para 11 of Part 1 of Schedule 2 of the Legal Aid in Criminal and Care Proceedings (Costs) Regulations.

Reasons for Decision

1. This is an appeal by Mr McNiff against the decision of Mr Collins, a Determining Officer at Norwich Crown Court, to refuse travelling expenses. Although Mr McNiff indicated in his notice of appeal that he wished to attend the hearing of his appeal and was sent notice of the hearing, he did not in fact turn up and accordingly I have decided the appeal on the papers.

2. Mr McNiff is in a large and well known chambers in London which specialises in criminal work and which has an annexe in Chelmsford. He was previously in chambers in Norwich and,

according to the Determining Officer's written reasons, he lives 16 miles from Norwich Crown Court.

3. Mr McNiff was instructed by Lucas & Wyllys, a firm of solicitors in Great Yarmouth, to represent David Comer who was charged with murder and attempting to pervert the course of justice. Two other defendants were also charged with the murder – the brutal killing of a 62 year old man by his drinking acquaintances. The other charge related to Comer's attempt to dispose of the murder weapon.

4. Following an 18 day trial at Norwich Crown Court, Comer was found not guilty of murder but guilty of attempting to pervert the course of justice, for which he was sentenced to nine months' imprisonment.

5. The representation order was granted on 24 September 2007 and therefore the determination of Mr McNiff's fees is governed by the Criminal Defence Service (Funding) Order 2007.

6. In addition to the graduated fee, Mr McNiff claimed travelling expenses to court of £585 consisting of 26 return train fares of £22.50 each, which the Determining Officer disallowed.

7. Paragraph 24 of schedule 1 to the 2007 Funding Order provides:

> "Where an advocate is instructed to appear in a court which is not within 40 kilometres of his office or chambers, the appropriate officer may allow an amount for travelling and other expenses incidental to that appearance, provided that the amount must not be greater than the amount, if any, which would be payable to a trial advocate from the nearest local Bar or the nearest advocate's office (whichever is the nearer) unless the advocate instructed to appear has obtained prior approval under CDS Regulations for the incurring of such expenses or can justify his attendance having regard to all the relevant circumstances of the case."

8. The wording of that paragraph derives from para 11 of Part 1 to Schedule 2 of the Legal Aid in Criminal and Care Proceedings (Costs) Regulations 1989,[1] but there are significant differences.

9. It seems to me that an appropriate way to break down para 24 would be:

(i) *if* an advocate is instructed to appear in a court which is not within 40 kilometres of his office or chambers *(the condition)*

(ii) the appropriate officer *may* allow an amount for travelling and other expenses *(the discretion)*

(iii) *provided* that the amount allowed must not be greater than the amount, if any, which would be payable to a trial advocate from the nearest local Bar or the nearest advocate's office (whichever is the nearer) *(the proviso)*

unless:
  (a) the advocate instructed to appear has obtained prior approval under CDS Regulations for the incurring of such expenses; or
  (b) the advocate can justify his attendance having regard to all the relevant circumstances of the case *(the disengagement of the proviso).*

10. In the present case it is not in issue that Mr McNiff was *instructed to appear in a court which is not within 40 kilometres of his ... chambers* thereby satisfying the condition in (i). Nor is it in issue that no prior approval was obtained from the Legal Services Commission for incurring the expenses, thereby ruling out the disengagement of the proviso by (iii)(a).

11. It seems to me that the issues are:

(1) Does the proviso (iii) apply? Is the amount claimed *greater than the amount, if any, which would be payable to a trial advocate from the nearest local Bar or the nearest advocate's office (whichever is the nearer)*?

(2) If so, is the proviso then disengaged on the ground (iii)(b) that Mr McNiff *can justify his attendance having regard to all the relevant circumstances of the case.*

12. The Determining Officer concluded that there is a local Bar in Norwich. In his written reasons he set out some statistics, some of which Mr McNiff disputes. Where there is a dispute – such as here, as to who does what work in Norwich – I am simply not in a position to make findings of fact. In the event, and for reasons which I explain below, it is not necessary for me to do so.

13. What is not in issue would appear to include: that there are four court rooms at Norwich Crown Court and one at King's Lynn; and there are two barristers' chambers in Norwich (East Anglian and Octagon House), both of which have members who practise in the Crown Court.

14. In his written reasons the Determining Officer explained:

"Both the regulations and guidance make no mention of the size of the local bar, simply that travelling expenses are not allowable where there is a local bar, and Norwich does have a local bar. This point was taken to the Taxing Master in 1996, (SCTO references 41/96 and 338/96). In both instances, in respect of travelling, the appeals were dismissed."

15. The two decisions referred to are decisions of Master Rogers on appeal by the same counsel. In *R v Carpenter* [41/96] Master Rogers upheld the Determining Officer's decision to refuse the travelling expenses to Norwich of counsel from London. The Determining Officer had concluded that there was a local Bar in Norwich and that it would have been quite possible for that defendant to have been represented by local counsel. Master Rogers concluded that counsel had failed to justify his attendance having regard to all the relevant circumstances of the case and continued:

"Counsel's main complaint seems to be against the so called Local Bar rule. This may be, as he suggests, restrictive but that is a matter to be addressed by the Bar authorities and, if appropriate, by way of amendment to the regulations, and this is not the appropriate case to seek to 'break' that so called rule."

In *R v Willard* [338/96] Master Rogers concluded that counsel had again failed to justify his attendance in preference to counsel from the local bar in Norwich.

16. In the present case the Determining Officer very properly and sensibly sought the view of the Resident Judge at Norwich Crown Court, His Honour Judge Jacobs, and quoted the response in his written reasons:

"The local chambers Octagon has six highly experienced practitioners who are regularly briefed in all cases including class 1 and that East Anglian has two such practitioners. There is a healthy local bar."

17. Having found that there is a local Bar in Norwich and that the proviso was therefore engaged, the Determining Officer concluded that this was not an appropriate case in which to allow travelling expenses.

18. Like the appellant in *R v Carpenter*, Mr McNiff's principal complaint would appear to be the finding that there is a local Bar in

Norwich. In his grounds of appeal he accepts the comments of HH Judge Jacobs (except presumably the last sentence), save that he considers that there are seven highly experienced practitioners in Octagon House rather than six. He submits that nine people are insufficient "to service a Tier 1, five court centre, dealing with a caseload now in excess of 1,000 cases, spread over 1,019 sitting days".

19. The grounds of appeal refer me to the decision of Sachs J (as he then was) in *Self* v *Self* [1954] P 480 and a comment that in order for there to be a local bar it would or should be recognised by the relevant Circuit. Mr McNiff submitted that there is no such recognition of a Norwich Bar. There is no Norwich Bar Mess, although there is an East Anglian Bar Mess. In fact I cannot find the comment he contends for in the report. On the contrary Sachs J said:

> "From the material put before me today it appears that there are at most three counsel practising at Brighton. Whether or not these three counsel technically do or do not constitute a local Bar for purposes such as the County Court Rules is, to my mind, irrelevant."

Although probably now of only historical interest, I observe that counsel in that case referred the court to the Annual Statement of the Bar:

> "The Council consider that in order to constitute a 'local bar' ... it is reasonable to require that not less than four practising members of the Bar willing to accept briefs in the county courts should occupy chambers in the locality."

20. The grounds of appeal then go on to draw distinctions between cities such as Norwich, with only a few barristers practising in the criminal courts, and cities such as Liverpool and Birmingham with large legal communities. The latter, Mr McNiff submitted, more obviously fall with the definition of "local Bar", were recognised as local Bars by their respective circuits, and each had is own Bar mess – unlike Norwich.

21. "Local bar" is not defined in the Funding Order. However some limited assistance can I think be gained from the wording of para 24: *would be payable to a trial advocate from the nearest local Bar or the nearest advocate's office (whichever is the nearer).* "Advocate" is defined in the Funding Order as:

"a barrister, a solicitor advocate or a solicitor who is exercising their automatic rights of audience in the Crown Court: Art 2."

If one juxtaposes "local Bar" with "solicitor's office", that might suggest a fairly modest number of practitioners could constitute a local Bar.

22. I am not sure that the existence of a Bar Mess can be a prerequisite for a local Bar. For example Cambridge has a Bar Mess, but only one set of Chambers. I suspect that the presence of a Bar Mess is more a reflection of history and the personalities of those who have been involved, than a formal recognition by the profession.

23. I do not think that the statistics quoted in Mr McNiff's grounds of appeal assist me. The existence of a local bar could not be the product of an equation involving the amount of work locally and the number of local practitioners. In the absence of a numerical or other definition, whether the barristers based in Norwich will amount to a "local Bar" will be a question of "feel". The best evidence of "feel" before me must be the view of the Resident Judge that: "there is a healthy local bar".

24. Accordingly in my judgment there is a local Bar in Norwich and the proviso in para 24 is therefore engaged. The Determining Officer cannot allow to Mr McNiff travelling expenses in a sum greater than that which would be allowed to an advocate from the nearest local Bar (Norwich) unless the proviso is disengaged. As the chambers in Norwich are within walking distance of the Crown Court, no sum would be allowed to a member of those chambers for the expense of travelling to the court.

25. Although not directly relevant to my decision I observe that the proviso could also be engaged by the presence of a local "advocate's office". It seems to me that the effect of the words in parentheses "whichever is the nearer" makes the presence of an advocate's office as relevant to the cap imposed by the proviso as the presence of a local bar, even if the claim for travelling expenses is being made by a barrister. Thus if I am wrong and there is no local Bar in Norwich, the proviso would still be engaged in relation to Mr McNiff's claim if there is an advocate's office (i.e. the office of a solicitor with rights of audience in the Crown Court) in Norwich or nearer to Norwich than Mr McNiff. While there is no evidence before me, I would be surprised if there is not an advocate's office in Norwich.

26. Is the proviso then disengaged on the ground that Mr McNiff can justify his attendance having regard to all the relevant circumstances of the case?

27. The difficulty here is that Mr McNiff's focus of attention is on the existence of a "local Bar" – a focus which may be misplaced as a result of the change in the wording of the regulation by the introduction of a local advocate's office as an alternative basis for engaging the proviso. Mr McNiff wants to argue that the local Bar is of insufficient size to service the criminal work in Norwich. Indeed at para 6.3 of his grounds of appeal, he explains:

> "My motivation is simple. Recent changes have made costs actually incurred by counsel in serving courts such as Norwich a very real and pressing issue. Indeed, for some (and the number is growing) it is the main obstacle for attending Norwich. The costs are being routinely disallowed because it is said there is a local bar and yet those who practice in Norwich could not sensibly cope, unaided, with the total workload of the court."

28. It seems to me that the purpose of para 24 is to limit travelling expenses to those that would be charged by the local practitioner unless the distant practitioner claiming them can justify his instruction. To my mind that seems perfectly sensible. However because of the focus on the principle of whether there is a local bar, the grounds of appeal do not attempt to justify Mr McNiff's attendance in this case. I do not know therefore whether there would have been counsel in local Chambers willing and able to be instructed in this case. The Resident Judge's comment would suggest that there are counsel in Norwich who are capable of conducting murder trials. But I do not know whether any of them would have been available.

29. Accordingly in my judgment Mr McNiff has not justified his attendance and the proviso has not been disengaged. The Determining Officer was right to limit Mr McNiff's travelling expenses to those that would have been payable to an advocate practising in Norwich – i.e. nil.

30. If I am wrong on that, then it seems to me that Mr McNiff could only be entitled to expenses that he has actually incurred, rather than some notional sum. The expenses which can be allowed are those "*incidental* to [the] appearance" (emphasis added). *The Oxford English Dictionary* (online ed.) defines "incidental" as:

"b. Of a charge or expense: Such as is incurred (in the execution of some plan or purpose) apart from the primary disbursements."

31. Thus if counsel travelled to court from home, he would be entitled to his travelling expenses from home (unless his Chambers were nearer to the court).

32. The appeal is dismissed.

Note

1. Where counsel is instructed to appear in a court which is not within 25 miles of his Chambers, the appropriate authority may allow an amount in respect of counsel's attendance at that court to cover any travelling and hotel expenses reasonably incurred and necessarily and exclusively attributable to counsel's attendance at that court, provided that the amount allowed shall not be greater than the amount, if any, which would be payable to counsel practising from the nearest local Bar unless counsel can justify his attendance having regard to all the relevant circumstances of the case.

Case 69
R
v
Ghaffar

[2009] 6 Costs LR 980

Supreme Court Costs Office
21 July 2009

Before:
Andrew Gordon-Saker, Costs Judge

Headnote

The costs judge in this appeal had to consider the proper application of the words, "the date fixed for the main hearing is changed by the court despite the advocate's objection" in para 18(1) of Schedule 4 to the Criminal Defence Service (Funding) Order, 2001, and held that counsel's "other commitment", could be an arranged holiday, and was not restricted to a clashing hearing, so that counsel became entitled to a "special preparation" fee.

Reasons for Decision

1. This is an appeal by Mr Ferm against the decision of Miss Hill, a Determining Officer, to disallow his claim for a wasted preparation fee.

2. Mr Ferm was instructed to represent Mohammed Ghaffar who was charged with perverting the course of justice. The charge arose out of a drugs related murder in Bradford.

3. The trial was fixed for 27 February 2007 with an estimated hearing length of 4–6 weeks. However that date was vacated on 7

February 2007 as a number of defendants were not ready. The judge, Holland J, proposed a new trial date of 4 June 2007 and directed that any submissions on the date should be made within seven days. On 8 February 2007 Mr Ferm wrote to the court explaining that he had booked (and paid for) a holiday abroad from 15 June to 23 June 2007. Despite his objection the trial went ahead on 6 June 2007 and Mr Ferm had to return his brief.

4. Mr Ferm claimed wasted preparation of 70 hours and relied on para 18(1) of Schedule 4 to the Criminal Defence Service (Funding) Order 2001:

> "A wasted preparation fee may be claimed where a trial advocate instructed in any case to which this paragraph applies is prevented from representing the assisted person in the main hearing by any of the following circumstances: ...
>
> (b) the date fixed for the main hearing is changed by the court despite the trial advocate's objection; ..."

5. In her written reasons the Determining Officer explained her decision in this way:

> "Counsel did *not* object to the date of the original fixture being vacated.
>
> His objections in relation to the proposed new date predated the actual fixing of that date. That date was *not* changed by the court.
>
> I am not satisfied that counsel's claim for wasted preparation can be said to come within any of the provisions of para 18, and accordingly consider that I have no statutory basis for authorising any payment for wasted preparation."

6. It seems to me that the only issue on this appeal is whether "the date fixed for the main hearing [was] changed by the court despite the trial advocate's objection". It cannot be in issue that the date was changed. Changing a fixture is a process – vacating the old and fixing the new. An objection to any part of the process is an objection to the change. Mr Ferm objected to a trial in June because he would be on holiday for two weeks. Despite his objection the date was changed to June. To my mind this falls absolutely squarely within sub-para 18(1)(b). Mr Ferm had objected to the change.

7. The Determining Officer goes on in her written reasons to explain her view that the provisions of para 18 relate only to

professional commitments and not holiday commitments but she does not give her reasons for reaching that view. In fact sub-paragraph 18(1)(a) covers a clash of professional commitments and 18(1)(e) covers a clash with judicial or other public commitments. I cannot see any reason to place a restriction on the words in sub-paragraph 18(1)(b). Had the draftsman intended the sub-paragraph to relate only to professional commitments there is no reason why he could not have said so.

8. Clearly counsel must be entitled to holidays. Clearly they should not book holidays for periods when they have existing professional commitments. But if, having booked a holiday, a trial is moved to that period despite their objection, I can see no reason to deprive them of payment for the work that they have done. As Mr Ferm made clear in his claim, his holiday was booked only after assurances by the Recorder of Leeds that the trial would not move under any circumstances.

9. In her written reasons the Determining Officer accepted that counsel had done substantial preparation. Having looked at the papers lodged by Mr Ferm I am satisfied that his claim for 70 hours is reasonable and accordingly the appeal is allowed in full.

Case 70
R
v
Newport

[2009] 6 Costs LR 983

Supreme Court Costs Office
3 September 2009

Before:
C. Campbell, Costs Judge

_____**Headnote**_____

Two issues arose on this appeal. The first was whether there were "exceptional circumstances" justifying a long delay by an advocate in submitting his claim for payment, where the delay was due to dishonest conduct by his clerk, rather than any oversight by the advocate himself. The second issue was whether where counsel had taken silk before the hearing, but the representation order had not been altered to permit instruction of a silk, but remained for two junior counsel, counsel could not be paid at all. The costs judge, following the earlier decision in *R* v *Duzgun and Another* [2000] 2 Costs LR 316, held that counsel could be paid as a leading junior.

Reasons for Decision

1. This is an appeal by Jonathan Laidlaw QC against two decisions made by the Determining Officer set out in the reasons of the Regional Taxing Manager dated 3 July 2009. Two points arise on the appeal. Firstly, whether the appellant should be given leave to request a

redetermination out of time; and secondly, whether Mr Laidlaw's fees for appearing for the defendant, Duncan Newport, in the Wolverhampton County Court should be allowed in the sum claimed (£28,919) or in the figure assessed by the Determining Officer which was £nil.

2. The factual background is that Newport had been convicted on 30 April 2004 of a single count of conspiracy to import cocaine from Columbia. He was sentenced to 26 years' imprisonment by His Honour Judge Woods QC. Mr Laidlaw had appeared for Newport at the trial, for which he submitted a red corner claim for a basic fee of £20,650, together with two half day refreshers at £300 each and one full day refresher of £600. In addition, Mr Laidlaw sought payment for various conferences and consultations. His claim was received by the National Taxing Team on 27 February 2006, and, as I have said, was assessed at nil. The reason for the assessment at this figure was that the representation order, which was dated 21 October 2004, said this:

> "**Duncan Robert Newport**
>
> Representation was granted for proceedings before the Crown Court ...
>
> The representation granted shall consist of representative solicitor, junior Counsel and Queen's Counsel including advice on preparation of the case for the proceedings ..."

3. Although Mr Laidlaw has subsequently taken Silk, at the time of the trial he was not in Silk, and accordingly the Determining Officer declined to award him a fee, because the representation order was never amended to cover two junior counsel rather than a silk and junior.

4. The Determining Officer's decision is dated 11 May 2006. However, for the reasons to which I shall refer, the letter in question did not come to Mr Laidlaw's notice until much later. By the time that he applied for redetermination on 15 June 2009, his application was seriously out of time, and the Regional Taxing Manager declined to entertain it. His reasons are dated 3 July 2009 and say this:

> "Having considered your further request I do not consider that exceptional circumstances have been made out to re-open the claim and allow redetermination ... The matter at that time [3 October 2006] was obviously in the forefront of counsel's mind but no further action ensued following that letter. Costs judges have frequently stated that

practitioners must have suitable systems in place not only to ensure the timely submission of claims in accordance with the Regulations/Funding Order but to also ensure that there were provisions in place to identify and meet the time limits for other actions, i.e., redetermination and where appropriate requests for written reasons. I therefore decline to redetermine the decision of Mr Tomlinson to refuse payment."

5. Ms Emily Dumett of counsel appeared before me at the appeal. On behalf of Mr Laidlaw, she accepted that there had been a delay in requesting redetermination, but submitted that there were exceptional circumstances to which the court should give due weight. Whilst it was right that the Determining Officer had refused payment as long ago as 11 May 2006, Mr Laidlaw had trusted his then senior clerk, a Mr Richard Fowler, to ensure that the claim and any appeal procedure had been appropriately and punctually conducted. Mr Laidlaw had made regular enquiries as to the progress of the claim. Unfortunately he had been deliberately misled as to the reasons for the delay. Mr Fowler had not informed him that the claim had been refused outright, still less the reasons for that refusal, nor of the contents of any correspondence between the parties. Instead, Mr Fowler had told Mr Laidlaw that the Taxing Team was "sorting things out". It was not until Mr Fowler had left Chambers (it was not said during the course of argument but I infer that his departure was "under a cloud") that the true position became known. In terms, Mr Laidlaw had been deceived by his clerk and told a pack of lies about the determination of the claim. Accordingly this was not a case where Mr Laidlaw had forgotten about the papers, nor was it an oversight, or a situation of human error. On the contrary, Mr Laidlaw had relied on his clerk and had been deceived. For a clerk to have deceived counsel in this way was, in Ms Dumett's submission, an "exceptional circumstance" and it was just on the facts that time should be extended so that redetermination could take place out of time.

6. It is clear from the circumstances I have described that the delay in this case has been significant. It has been stated on many occasions by costs judges and elsewhere that barristers must have suitable systems in place which ensure that claims for fees and requests for redetermination are made within the time limit set out in the Legal Aid in Criminal and Care Proceedings (Costs) Regulations 1989 as amended. In the present case, had this been a situation in which Mr

Laidlaw had put aside the papers because of "pressures of work" I would not consider the circumstances to have been exceptional. However, that was not the situation here. On the contrary, this was a rare and most regrettable situation where Mr Laidlaw, and presumably other members of his Chambers, had been deceived by their clerk and been given information that was plainly false, as the clerk well knew. It follows that I consider that exceptional circumstances have been made out, and that the Determining Officer must redetermine the claim out of time.

7. The second limb of the appeal relates to the representation order. It is a fact that at the date the order was made, Mr Laidlaw was not in silk. Accordingly (and he accepts) no claim can be advanced on the basis that he should receive the level of fees that a Silk could justify on taxation. That said, Mr Laidlaw submits that the entire disallowance of his fees for the trial is unjust. Instead, the Determining Officer ought to have allowed payment at the rate which junior counsel would have been paid had the representation order been amended to cover two junior counsel rather than leading and junior counsel. In this submission, Ms Dumett relies on the decision of Master Rogers in *Duzgun and Another* [2000] 2 Costs LR 316. In that case, the legal aid order covered two counsel, but had not been amended to authorise the instruction of leading counsel. On taxation the Determining Officer refused to allow any fee for the leading counsel, who had claimed payment under the certificate. On page 323 Master Rogers said this:

> "However there is a second string to his [Mr Boney's] bow, which is that even if he is not entitled to be paid as leading counsel, he is at least entitled to be paid at the rate of junior counsel. The basis for that argument is that the valid legal aid order in writing does cover two counsel, and only one counsel has so far been paid for it is quite clear that two counsel represented the defendant at trial."

8. Later, on page 324, Master Rogers said this:

> "I see nothing in the Regulations that prevents a QC from making a claim for payment only as leading junior counsel. The circumstances on which a QC may wish to do this will obviously be few and far between but clearly in this particular case it is such an example and I do not feel that the Regulations prevent me from coming to the conclusion which I

think justice demands, namely that some payment is made to Mr Boney for his representation of Mr Duzgun."

9. In the present case, Ms Dumett relies on Master Rogers' decision as authority for the proposition that where, as here, the legal aid authority covered two counsel, Mr Laidlaw should not go unpaid because he was not, at the time, in silk, but that, on the contrary, he should be remunerated on the basis of a junior counsel.

10. In his written reasons, the Regional Taxing Manager has adopted a strict approach:

> "In the instant case the representation specified junior and Queen's counsel. Mr Brassington was rightly remunerated as the junior but as Mr Laidlaw had not at the time become Queen's counsel there is and was no provision to remunerate him under the terms of the representation order in place."

11. In strict terms, the Regional Taxing Manager is correct, but in my judgment, such an outcome would be unjust and, as Master Rogers observed in *Duzgun*, authority was given for payment of two counsel, but only one so far has been paid. In these circumstances, it is my view that justice demands that some payment should be made for a second counsel, given that the representation order contemplated payment of such a counsel, albeit that this will be at the rate applicable for a junior counsel rather than for a Silk.

12. For these reasons the appeal will be allowed. The Determining Officer must redetermine the claim, but on the basis that any fee allowed should be paid at a rate befitting a junior counsel rather than a leading counsel. That said, I do not consider that counsel has come out of this matter unblemished; despite the failings of his clerk, at the end of the day counsel is responsible not only for checking that the correct representation order is in place, but also that his administrative affairs are being handled competently by his clerks. In the circumstances I consider that a penalty of 5% should be applied to any sum payable following the redetermination. Provided Mr Laidlaw is content to accept such a penalty, the appeal will be allowed on the terms I have set out and for the reasons I have given.

Case 71

R

v

Islami

[2009] 6 Costs LR 988

Senior Courts Costs Office
6 October 2009

Before:
C Campbell, Costs Judge

Headnote

This was the second time that this matter had been brought before the costs judge. On the first occasion, the costs judge allowed an appeal against the total disallowance of a solicitor's bill for £58,060.13, which had been lodged three years nine months late, on the ground that such disallowance would be disproportionate, and substituted a 5% penalty. Unhappily, the solicitor then took another nine months before re-lodging the bill, and the Determining Officer did not accept the solicitor's stated reason for that further delay and again totally disallowed the bill. On this occasion, the costs judge dismissed the appeal save as to the disbursement element of the bill, which had been paid by the solicitor six years earlier.

Reasons for Decision

1. This is an appeal by Michael Carroll & Co Solicitors against the decision of the Determining Officer dated 7 May 2009 to disallow the entirety of the appellant's claim for their work on behalf of the defendant, Ismet Islami, in the Wood Green Crown Court on the grounds that:

"The case concluded on 19 December 2003 over five years ago ... it is not reasonable to seek to justify a further considerable delay and your explanation, in any event, does not constitute special circumstances."

2. For these reasons the Determining Officer declined to determine the claim, which sought the sum of £58,069.13 including disbursements.

3. Regrettably this is not the first occasion on which the appellant has appealed pursuant to para 21(1) and (2) of Schedule 1 of the Criminal Defence Service (Funding) Order 2001 as amended. As the Determining Officer has stated, the case which had involved a broad set of allegations against Islami including rape, kidnap, false imprisonment and facilitating the illegal entry into the UK of two foreign nationals, was disposed of on 19 December 2003, following a three month trial and acquittal on all counts. Accordingly, under para 11 to Schedule 1 of the Order, the claim should have been submitted for determination within three months of that date, namely by 10 March 2004. In the event it was not lodged with the National Taxing Team until December 2007 by which time it was three years and nine months late.

4. In written reasons dated 1 April 2008, the Determining Officer stated that he could find no good reason or exceptional circumstances why the time limit should be extended and accordingly the entire claim for £58,060.13 was disallowed. Dissatisfied, the appellant appealed to me, and at an oral hearing on 4 June 2008 I was persuaded that although the claim had been submitted seriously late (which the appellant accepted) the disallowance of the entire claim would be a disproportionate penalty. The paid disbursements alone amounted to £8,462.09 in addition to which the appellant had spent £1,095.20 on travelling expenses. In dealing with the appeal I was also mindful of the Note distributed to practitioners by the Regional Taxing Manager that from 2 January 2007 all claims received by the appropriate NTT region would be subject to the application of consistent criteria with regard to time limits. In relation to "out of time claims" the guidance to be found on HM Courts Service website says this:

"All financial penalties including refusal to determine will be directed to profit costs and not 'other' disbursements ... examples of exceptional circumstances may include; profit costs substantial and a refusal to tax would be a disproportionate sanction."

5. With this guidance in mind, I decided that total disallowance was a disproportionate penalty, and I directed that the bill should be determined albeit that a 5% penalty should be applied to the sum ultimately allowed by the Determining Officer. To that extent the appeal succeeded.

6. Although my reasons did not say so in terms, in my opinion it was implicit that the appellant should attend to the mechanics of determination of its claim as a matter of urgency and priority.

7. My decision was dated 2 July 2008, but it was not until 30 March 2009 that the application for determination of the claim was re-submitted to the National Taxing Team. In a letter dated 15 April 2009 to the appellant, the Determining Officer requested the appellant to explain why an additional nine months had elapsed from the date of the decision which had thereby contributed to an already excessive delay. By letter dated 29 April 2009 the appellant replied to the Determining Officer in the following terms:

> "A telephone call was received from yourself last year advising that the National Taxing Team were shutting its office in Bloomsbury. A member of the administrative staff was asked to send a box of papers containing the claim. It was assumed that this was done.
>
> During that person's recent extensive sick leave we discovered that she had not in fact sent the claim for costs. Once this was realised we immediately submitted the claim for costs. The failure to submit the claim was not noted due to other large claims being paid and it was during the year end reconciliation that we discovered she had not submitted the claim."

8. For his part, the Determining Officer did not accept that the reasons set out in the letter of 29 April 2009 constituted a good reason for the delay, still less were there any exceptional circumstances. He expressed the view that I had already taken any exceptional circumstances justifying determination out of time into account when I made my decision on July 2 last year. In these circumstances it was not reasonable to seek to justify a further considerable delay, and for that reason he refused to determine the claim.

9. At the appeal Mr Carroll appeared on behalf of his firm. He informed me that after my decision of 2 July 2008 had been received by his firm, a telephone call had been taken from the National Taxing

Team stating that the Bloomsbury office of the NTT was closing. In these circumstances, Mr Carroll made arrangements with a member of his firm for the papers to be dispatched. It had been his belief that this had been done. However, on 12 February 2009 the member of staff in question had gone off work on long term sickness at which point various issues about work she had undertaken had come to light. This included the fact that the claim had not been submitted to the National Taxing Team after all. Subsequently the employee in question has left the employment of the appellant.

10. Mr Carroll submitted that if the claim is disallowed, it is the firm that will suffer and that the absence of payment in this particular case had not been picked up immediately because the firm had lodged several claims which meant that payments were received into the firm's office account at regular intervals sufficient to cover outgoings. A further factor was that in the past, claims had taken over six months to be processed by the NTT and it had been reasonable to assume that this might be the case with regard to the papers in *R v Islami*.

11. Having considered Mr Carroll's submissions with care, I regret to say that I do not find them persuasive, albeit that I recognise the difficulties which face small firms which undertake publicly funded criminal cases. In the appellant's submissions for the first appeal, Mr Carroll submitted that many small legal aid firms are struggling to survive and that the loss of £58,000 "in such stricken times" would bear very heavily on his practice. Whilst I have sympathy with that submission, the fact is that the remedy lies in the hands of the appellant firm itself, and if an amount of £58,000 was of such significance, I would have expected not only that the claim be submitted as soon as possible after 2 July 2008, but also that progress on the determination be followed up. Regrettably this did not happen; it appears that the task of re-lodging the papers was entrusted to an employee who proved to be unreliable and that no check of any nature was made to ensure that the correct papers had been received by the Determining Officer and that the determination was in progress. I should add in this respect that the Determining Officer in question, Mr Nevett had earlier indicated he would support any request made by the appellant to expedite the appeal and, as I have said, he also contacted the firm after it had been heard to alert Mr Carroll that the NTT would be moving from Bloomsbury. Put shortly, in my judgment there has been yet another failing by the firm with regard to its internal

administration and I agree with the Determining Officer that this explanation does not amount to "good reason" why the time limit for lodging the claim should yet again be extended.

12. This leads to the second point; is total disallowance a disproportionate penalty sufficient to constitute an "exceptional circumstance"? On the last occasion, I decided that the dead loss of £58,000 was a disproportionate sanction, even allowing for the then already serious delay. In making my decision I took into account Mr Carroll's submission that such a loss would have substantial consequences for the firm. Fifteen months on, have those circumstances changed in the sense that the dead loss of £58,000 would no longer be exceptional? On the present facts, I am no longer persuaded that total disallowance of profit costs would be a disproportionate sanction. As I have said, if the sum of £58,000 had been needed with the urgency urged on me at the hearing on 4 June 2008, I would have expected the claim to have been re-lodged straightaway and for it to be carefully "tracked" with Mr Nevett who had previously indicated his willingness to expedite matters where necessary. Instead, it is plain that the administrative problems which I identified at the first appeal, were not resolved with the result that if I allow the appeal and direct the Determining Officer to determine the claim, the work in question will need to be done nearly six years after the date of disposal and several years since the Determining Officer who determined the related claims in this case, retired from the NTT. Weighing these factors, in my judgment the loss of the firm's profit costs do not now constitute "exceptional circumstances", and I uphold the Determining Officer's decision on this point.

13. So far as disbursements are concerned, these are sums which the appellant expended out of the office account over six years ago. Mr Carroll told me that no prior authority had been granted, as it had been necessary in a number of instances (e.g. employment of interpreters) to pay "up front". In my view, the determination of such disbursements, even after all this time, can still be carried out without loss of fairness. I therefore direct that the Determining Officer should determine the disbursements without penalty. For the avoidance of doubt, and so that there is no further delay, the appellant must lodge the necessary papers within 14 days of receipt of these reasons, otherwise the claim will not be determined. To the extent indicated, the appeal is allowed.

Case 72
R
v
Phillips

[2009] 6 Costs LR 993

Senior Courts Costs Office
12 November 2009

Before:
Andrew Gordon-Saker, Costs Judge

Headnote

In this appeal, the costs judge was again concerned with the distinction between a "cracked trial" and a "guilty plea", but had to construe what if any difference was caused by the draftsman's insertion of the additional word "either" in the definition of a cracked trial in para 1 of Schedule 2 to the Criminal Defence Service (Funding) Order 2007 for the purposes of calculating the appropriate litigator's graduated fee scheme, which does not appear in the corresponding definition in the 2001 Funding Order.

Reasons for Decision

1. This is an appeal by Broomhead & Saul, a firm of solicitors in Ilminster, against the calculation of a litigator graduated fee by the Legal Services Commission.

2. The solicitors were instructed to represent Damon Phillips who was charged with causing grievous bodily harm in case number T2008 7035 and was charged with assault occasioning actual bodily harm in case number T2008 0146.

3. In case 7035 (GBH) Phillips pleaded not guilty at a plea and case management hearing on 13 June 2008 and the trial was listed for 29 September 2008.

4. Case 0146 (ABH) was listed for a plea and case management hearing on 17 October 2008. However a basis of plea in case 7035 was agreed and case 0146 was mentioned at the hearing on 29 September 2008. On that day, a formal not guilty plea was entered in case 0146 and, on a subsequent date, the court ordered that the charge should lie on the file.

5. In respect of case 0146 the solicitors claimed a graduated fee on the basis that it was a cracked trial. However the fee allowed was calculated on the basis that it was a guilty plea. It is against that decision that the solicitors now appeal. The solicitors requested that the appeal be dealt with on the papers rather than at a hearing. The Lord Chancellor has made written representations to ensure that the public interest is taken into account and the solicitors have responded in writing to those submissions. I have not therefore had the benefit of any oral argument.

6. Paragraph 1 of Schedule 2 to the Criminal Defence Service (Funding) Order 2007 provides these definitions:

"'cracked trial' means a case on indictment in which –

(a) a plea and case management hearing takes place and –

   (i) the case does not proceed to trial (whether by reason of pleas of guilty or for other reasons) or the prosecution offers no evidence; and

   (ii) either –

(aa) in respect of one or more counts to which the assisted person pleaded guilty, he did not so plead at the plea and case management hearing; or

(bb) in respect of one or more counts which did not proceed, the prosecution did not, before or at the plea and case management hearing, declare an intention of not proceeding with them; or

(b) the case is listed for trial without a plea and case management hearing taking place;

'guilty plea' means a case on indictment which –

(a) is disposed of without a trial because the assisted person pleaded guilty to one or more counts; and

(b) is not a cracked trial."

7. Sub-paragraph 2(5) of Schedule 2 provides:

"For the purposes of this Schedule, a case on indictment which discontinues at or before the plea and case management hearing otherwise than –

(a) by reason of a plea of guilty being entered, or

(b) in accordance with sub-paragraph (3) of this paragraph,

must be treated as a guilty plea.

(Sub-paragraph (3) deals with sent cases that are discontinued or dismissed.)"

8. It is not in issue that, as Phillips did not plead guilty, this case cannot fall within the definition of a "guilty plea" provided by para 1. However the Lord Chancellor submits that this case falls within sub-paragraph 2(5) and must therefore be treated as a guilty plea. It is submitted that the case cannot fall within the definition of a "cracked trial" provided by para 1 because the prosecution declared an intention of not proceeding before or at the plea and case management hearing.

9. I have been provided with copies of the transcripts for the relevant hearings, which show:

29 September 2008 – Phillips pleaded guilty to causing grievous bodily harm (7035) and not guilty to assault occasioning actual bodily harm (0146). In relation to 0146, prosecuting counsel told the court:

"The Crown and defence have discussed how that will be disposed of at the end of these proceedings."

Sentencing in 7035 was adjourned pending reports and Phillips was remanded in custody.

23 October 2008 – Prosecuting counsel (Mr Large) who had appeared at the previous hearing was not available. Counsel who then appeared for the Crown, Mr Askham, was "concerned that Mr Large is not here because it may be that the court will want to know why he proposed or proposes taking a certain course in relation to" 0146. Mr Askham's instructions were "that [Mr Large] will ... ask for the other matter [0146] to remain on the court file". Miss Bradberry, counsel for the defence, explained:

> "... I approached Mr Large and simply said what is the prosecution's bottom line in terms of the basis of plea *and it was communicated back that the ABH matter was to lie on the file and that was the basis upon which Mr Phillips entered the guilty plea on the grievous bodily harm offence* and that was, he was seen in custody. That was agreed.
>
> I was aware ... when Mr Phillips entered the guilty plea to the grievous bodily harm and the not guilty plea to the ABH that there were concerns raised at that stage by the prosecution but certainly on behalf of the defence *I made it clear that that was the offer that was given and that was the offer that was accepted* and at that point in court Mr Large, once the pleas had been entered, stated that the issue of the grievous bodily, the ABH would be resolved at the end of this trial and the court was not to take any action with regard to the fixing of the trial or take any further action." (emphasis added)

The judge expressed concern and the matter was adjourned to await the return of Mr Large.

28 October 2008 – Mr Large apologised for the confusion and explained:

> "When the defendant agreed to enter a guilty plea to the s 18 indictment [7035] for which he is to be sentenced today the Crown agreed that the other indictment would lie on the file ..."

10. To my mind it is clear, from the explanation given by Miss Bradberry on 23 October 2008 and from the explanation given by Mr Large on 28 October 2008, that agreement had been reached before the hearing on 29 September 2008 that Phillips would plead guilty to the GBH charge (7035) and that the prosecution would not proceed with the ABH charge (0146); and that it was on that basis that Phillips changed his plea to guilty to the GBH charge on 29 September 2008.

11. In view of that agreement, I cannot reach a conclusion other than that the prosecution declared an intention of not proceeding with the ABH charge (0146) before the plea and case management hearing on 29 September 2008.

12. In their response to the Lord Chancellor's submissions the solicitors contend:

"... once it has been established that a PCMH has taken place and for whatever reason the matter does not then proceed to trial the criteria for a cracked trial is fulfilled ... where either ...

(a) (aa) in respect of one or more counts to which the assisted person pleaded guilty, he did not so plead at the plea and case management hearing; or

(b) (bb) in respect of one or more counts which did not proceed, the prosecution did not, before or at the plea and case management hearing, declare an intention of not proceeding with them."

13. I must confess to some difficulty with the wording of the definition of "cracked trial" in para 1. In the ordinary way one would assume that the intended effect would be that identified by Lloyd Jones J in *Lord Chancellor v Frieze* [2007] EWHC 1490 (QB), a case concerned with advocates' graduated fees under the 2001 Funding Order. After setting out the definition of "cracked trial" the learned judge said:

"5. The effect of these provisions is that where there is a guilty plea or a decision by the prosecution not to proceed after the plea and case management hearing ('PCMH'), or after listing for trial if there is no PCMH, the case should be paid for as a cracked trial and not as a guilty plea. However, if the guilty plea or decision not to proceed is made before or at the PCMH, then the case is to be paid for as a plea.

6. On the face of the provision there seems to be a sensible basis for drawing the line in this way. In a situation where a guilty plea has not been entered by the time of the PCMH or the prosecution has not indicated that it does not intend to proceed by the time of the PCMH, then work will have to be done in preparation for trial and that should be reflected in the remuneration for the case."

14. Paragraph 9 of Schedule 4 to the Criminal Defence Service (Funding) Order 2001, the effect of which the learned judge was considering in *Frieze*, provided (insofar as material):

"(3) A case on indictment in which a pleas and directions hearing [or plea and case management hearing] takes place is a cracked trial if it fulfils the following conditions:

(a) the matter did not proceed to trial (whether by reason of pleas of guilty or for other reasons) or the prosecution offered no evidence, and

(b) (i) in respect of one or more counts to which the assisted person pleaded guilty, he did not so plead at the pleas and directions hearing [or plea and case management hearing]; or

(ii) in respect of one or more counts which were not proceeded with, the prosecution did not, before or at the pleas and directions hearing [or plea and case management hearing], declare an intention of not proceeding with them."

15. It would seem clear that Lloyd Jones J considered that "or" between sub-paragraphs b(i) and b(ii) was conjunctive:

"... where there is a guilty plea or a decision by the prosecution not to proceed after the plea and case management hearing ('PCMH') ... the case should be paid for as a cracked trial."

Thus a case would be a cracked trial under the 2001 Funding Order if

(a) a plea and case management hearing takes place; and
(b) it did not proceed to trial or the prosecution offered no evidence; and
(c) the defendant did not plead guilty at the plea and case management hearing; *and*
(d) the prosecution did not declare an intention not to proceed at or before the plea and case management hearing.

16. So, if this were a case to which the 2001 Funding Order applied, it would not be a cracked trial because the decision not to proceed was made before or at the plea and case management hearing:

"However, if the guilty plea *or* decision not to proceed is made before or at the PCMH, then the case is to be paid for as a plea: per Lloyd Jones J in *Frieze* (emphasis added)."

17. The wording of the definition of cracked trial in para 1 of Schedule 2 of the 2007 Funding Order is similar to that provided by the 2001 Funding Order, but the draftsman has added the word "either" between sub-paragraphs (a) and (b). ("Either" has also been added in the definition of cracked trial in Schedule 1 of the 2007 Funding Order, which concerns advocates' fees.)

18. "Either" can mean "each of the two" or "one or other of the two" (OED 2nd ed; 1989).

19. In the context of this paragraph it seems to me that "either" must mean "each of the two". The obvious intention is that if the case survives beyond the plea and case management hearing as a contested case which will need preparation towards trial, the litigator will be paid a higher fee than if the contest is settled before or at the plea and case management hearing.

20. As far as I can see there is no obvious reason why the draftsman would wish "either" to be construed as "one or other of the two". It would lead to the illogical result that if an assisted person pleads guilty at the plea and case management hearing, the litigator would be paid for a guilty plea, but if he pleads not guilty and the prosecution is abandoned at the plea and case management hearing (as here), the litigator would be paid for a cracked trial.

21. That would lead to a conflict with para 2(5) of Schedule 2 which provides that a case which discontinues at or before the plea and case management hearing otherwise than by reason of a guilty plea must be treated as a guilty plea.

22. In my judgment a case will be a cracked trial under the 2007 Funding Order in the same circumstances as it would be a cracked trial under the 2001 Funding Order, *viz* if:

(a) a plea and case management hearing takes place; and
(b) it did not proceed to trial or the prosecution offered no evidence; and
(c) the defendant did not plead guilty at the plea and case management hearing; *and*
(d) the prosecution did not declare an intention not to proceed at or before the plea and case management hearing,

23. As, in the present case, it was agreed before the plea and case management hearing that case 0146 would not be proceeded with, the case was not a cracked trial within the meaning of para 1(2) of Schedule 2 to the 2007 Funding Order and is payable under para 2(5) as a guilty plea.

24. Accordingly the appeal is dismissed.

25. In its response to the consultation conducted by the Ministry of Justice on the draft Criminal Defence Service (Funding) (Amendment

No. 2) Order 2007 (which introduced Litigators' graduated fees), the Law Society submitted:

"*Definition of cracked trial*

This clause is somewhat confusing, in particular (bb) seems to contain too many negatives for it easily to make sense. It would be helpful if the whole section could be re-drafted in a clear, intelligible way."

26. I agree. I fail to see why something similar to the wording in para 22 above could not have been employed. (I observe that in its response to the Law Society dated 14 December 2007 the Ministry suggested a need for consistency with the advocates' scheme which "has caused little difficulty in the past".)

Index

Ancillary orders in costs proceedings, 862–863
Barrister's clerk,
  dishonest conduct of,
    delay in submitting claim for payment, 983–987
Basic fee,
  "notional", 967–971
Claims handlers,
  trade unions, 886–905
Conditional fee agreements,
  withdrawal from, 931–966
Conflicting evidence,
  oral,
    costs judge's findings, 931–966
Cracked trial,
  distinguished from guilty plea, 993–1000
Delay,
  submitting claim for payment,
    dishonest conduct of barrister's clerk, 983–987
Dishonest conduct of barrister's clerk,
  delay in submitting claim for payment, 983–987
Disclosure, 868
  electronic disclosure, 906–930
  professional privilege, 869–870
Disproportionate penalty,
  exceptional circumstances, 988–992
Electronic disclosure, 906–930
Equal footing,
  unrepresented claimant, 906–930
Evidence,
  oral,
    costs judge's findings, 931–966
Exceptional circumstances,
  clerk's dishonesty, 983–987
  disproportionate penalty, 988–992
Factual issues,
  judicial determination of, 911–914
Graduated fee scheme,
  distinction between cracked trial and guilty plea, 993–1000
Guilty plea,
  distinguished from cracked trial, 993–1000
Holidays,
  hearing date changed to clash with, special preparation fee, 980–982
Housing trusts,
  as public authorities, 875–881
Impecunious claimant, 859–874
Implied term, 898–900
Indemnity costs order,
  where claimant succeeded only on minor claims, 882–885
Junior counsel,
  fee of,
    methods of calculating, 967–971
  takes silk,
    representation order not altered, 983–987
Limitation, 904–905
London barristers appearing in Norwich,
  travelling expenses, 972–979
London rates, 906–930
"Notional",
  basic fee, 967–971
Oral evidence,
  conflicting, 931–966

Index

Professional privilege, 869–870
   and disclosure, 868
Proportionality,
   unrepresented claimant, 906–930
Protective costs orders, 875–881
Public authorities,
   housing trusts, 875–881

Representation orders,
   junior counsel,
      not altered when counsel takes silk, 983–987

Special preparation fee,
   when hearing date changed to clash with holiday, 980–982

Third party costs awards, 859–874
   justice and proportionality, 870–873
   principles, 863–865
Trade unions,
   claims handlers, 886–905
Travelling expenses,
   London barristers appearing in Norwich, 972–979

Unconscionable bargain, 901–904
Unrepresented claimant,
   equal footing, 906–930
   proportionality, 906–930

Vibration white finger,
   claims handlers, 886–905

Index of Reported Cases
(1910–2009)

1-800 Flowers Inc v
Phonenames Ltd
[2001] 2 Costs LR 286
A B and Others v Leeds Teaching
Hospitals NHS Trust
(In the Matter of the Nationwide
Organ Group Litigation)
[2003] 3 Costs LR 405
A Local Authority v
A Mother and Child
[2001] 1 Costs LR 136
A v The Chief Constable
of South Yorkshire Police
[2008] 6 Costs LR 935
Aaron v Okoye
[1998] 2 Costs LR 6
Aaron v Shelton
[2004] 3 Costs LR 488
Abedi v Penningtons
[2000] 2 Costs LR 205
Admiral Management Services
Ltd v Para-Protect Europe Ltd
and Others
[2003] 1 Costs LR 1
Adrian Alan Ltd v Fuglers (a Firm)
[2003] 4 Costs LR 518
Aehmed and Others v The Legal
Services Commission
[2009] 3 Costs LR 425
Aerospace Publishing Ltd and
Another v Thames Water
Utilities Ltd
[2007] 3 Costs LR 389

Agassi v Robinson (HM Inspector of
Taxes) (Bar Council and Law
Society Intervening)
[2006] 2 Costs LR 283
Al Fayed v Hamilton and Others
[2002] 3 Costs LR 389
Ali and Others v Lord Chancellor's
Department
[2002] 2 Costs LR 258
Ali Reza-Delta Transport Co Ltd v
United Arab Shipping Co Sag
[2004] 1 Costs LR 18
Al-Koronky and Another v
Time-Life Entertainment Group
Ltd and Another
[2007] 1 Costs LR 57
Amber Construction Services Ltd v
London Interspace HG Ltd
[2008] 5 Costs LR 715
Amber v Stacey
[2001] 2 Costs LR 325
Andrews and In the Matter of the
Criminal Justice Act 1988
[1999] 2 Costs LR 133
Angel Airlines SA v Dean & Dean
(CA)
[2009] 2 Costs LR 182
Angel Airlines SA v Dean & Dean
(QBD)
[2009] 2 Costs LR 159
Angel Airlines SA v Dean & Dean
Solicitors
[2007] 3 Costs LR 355

Index of Reported Cases (1910–2009)

Anthony v Ellis & Fairbairn (a Firm)
[2000] 2 Costs LR 277

Apex Frozen Foods Ltd v Ali and Others
[2007] 6 Costs LR 818

Arkin v Borchard Lines Ltd and Others
[2005] 4 Costs LR 643

Arkin v Borchard Lines Ltd and Others (No. 2)
[2004] 2 Costs LR 231

Arkin v Borchard Lines Ltd and Others (No. 3)
[2004] 2 Costs LR 267

Armitage v Nurse
[2000] 2 Costs LR 231

Arrowfield Services Ltd v BP Collins (a Firm)
[2005] 2 Costs LR 171

Aspen Property Investment plc v Leslie Ratcliffe and Others
[1997] 2 Costs LR 1

Aspin v Metric Group Ltd
[2008] 2 Costs LR 259

Atack v Lee and Grechan; Ellerton v Harris
[2005] 2 Costs LR 308

B (Children)
[2005] 4 Costs LR 675

Bailey v IBC Vehicles Ltd
[1998] 2 Costs LR 46

Barndeal Ltd and Another v London Borough of Richmond-Upon-Thames
[2006] 1 Costs LR 47

Baxendale-Walker v The Law Society
[2006] 5 Costs LR 696

Baxendale-Walker v The Law Society
[2007] 3 Costs LR 475

Baylis v Kelly and Others
[1997] 2 Costs LR 54

BCCI v Ali and Others
[2000] 2 Costs LR 243

Begum v Klarit
[2005] 3 Costs LR 452

Bevan Ashford (a Firm) v Geoff Yeandle (Contractors) Ltd (in Liquidation)
[1998] 2 Costs LR 15

Biguzzi v Rank Leisure plc
[2000] 1 Costs LR 67

Bilkus v Stockler Brunton (a Firm)
[2009] 4 Costs LR 652

Bim Kemi AB v Blackburn Chemicals Ltd
[2004] 2 Costs LR 201

Birmingham City Council v Crook and Others
[2007] 5 Costs LR 732

Birmingham City Council v Forde
[2009] 2 Costs LR 206

Birmingham City Council v Lee
[2009] 2 Costs LR 191

Blackham v Entrepose UK
[2005] 1 Costs LR 68

Boodhoo (Harry), Solicitor (Re)
[2007] 3 Costs LR 433

Booth v Britannia Hotels Ltd
[2003] 1 Costs LR 43

Index of Reported Cases (1910–2009)

Botham v Niazi (sued as Imran Khan); Lamb v Niazi (sued as Imran Khan)
[2005] 2 Costs LR 259
Bourns Inc v Raychem Corporation
[1999] 1 Costs LR 27
Bourns Inc v Raychem Corporation & Latham & Watkins
[1999] 2 Costs LR 72
Bovis Homes Ltd v Kendrick Construction Ltd
[2009] 5 Costs LR 778
Boyd & Hutchinson v Joseph
[2003] 3 Costs LR 358
Brawley v Marczynski and Another
[2003] 3 Costs LR 325
Brawley v Marczynski and Business Lines Ltd
[2003] 1 Costs LR 53
Brewer v Secretary of State for Justice
[2009] 3 Costs LR 440
Brewer v The Supreme Court Costs Office
[2009] 3 Costs LR 462
Bridgewater v Griffiths
[1999] 2 Costs LR 52
Brisset v Brisset
[2009] 4 Costs LR 641
Bromsgrove Medical Products Ltd v Edgar Vaughan & Co Ltd
[1998] 1 Costs LR 75
Brown v MCASSO Music Productions
[2006] 3 Costs LR 404
Brush and Another v Bower Cotton & Bower (a Firm)
(1992) Costs LR (Core) 223

Bufton v Hill
[2002] 3 Costs LR 381
Burchell v Bullard and Others
[2005] 3 Costs LR 507
Burkett (R) v London Borough of Hammersmith and Fulham
[2005] 1 Costs LR 104
Burridge and Another v Stafford and Another; Khan v Ali
[2001] 1 Costs LR 77
Burstein v Times Newspapers Ltd
[2003] 1 Costs LR 111
Burton Marsden Douglas (a Firm), In the Matter of; Marsden and Douglas v Guide Dogs for the Blind Association and Others
[2004] 3 Costs LR 378
Business Environment Bow Lane Ltd v Deanwater Estates Ltd
[2009] 4 Costs LR 672
Butt v Nizami and Kamuluden
[2006] 3 Costs LR 483

C v Merseyside Regional Ambulance Service NHS Trust
[2004] 3 Costs LR 363
C v W
[2009] 1 Costs LR 123
Callery v Gray (HL)
[2002] 2 Costs LR 205
Callery v Gray (No. 1)
[2001] 2 Costs LR 163
Callery v Gray (No. 2)
[2001] 2 Costs LR 205
Campbell v MGN Ltd
[2006] 1 Costs LR 120

Index of Reported Cases (1910–2009)

Cantor Fitzgerald International and Another v Tradition (UK) Ltd and Others
[2003] 4 Costs LR 614

Capewell v Her Majesty's Revenue and Customs and Another
[2007] 2 Costs LR 287

Carver v BAA plc
[2008] 5 Costs LR 779

Cavaliere v Legal Services Commission
[2003] 3 Costs LR 350

Child Abduction and Custody Act 1985, In the Matter of the, and in the Matter of R (Minors) Taxation of Costs – Solicitors' Hourly Rate and Care and Conduct Mark Up
[1997] 1 Costs LR 1

Chohan v Times Newspaper Ltd
[2001] 1 Costs LR 127

Chohan v Times Newspapers Ltd
[2002] 1 Costs LR 1

Chrulew and Others v Borm-Reid & Co (a Firm)
(1991) Costs LR (Core) 150

CIBC Mellon Trust Company and Another v Stolzenberg and Others
[2005] 4 Costs LR 617

CIBC Mellon Trust Company Ltd and Another v Mora Hotel Corporation NY and Others
[2003] 3 Costs LR 334

Claims Direct Test Cases, In the Matter of
[2003] 2 Costs LR 254

Clifford Harris & Co v Solland International Ltd and Others
[2005] 3 Costs LR 414

Codent Ltd v Lyson Ltd
[2007] 2 Costs LR 185

Cole v British Telecommunications plc
[2000] 2 Costs LR 310

Colley v Council for Licensed Conveyancers
[2002] 1 Costs LR 147

Commissioners for Her Majesty's Revenue and Customs v Xicom Systems Ltd
[2009] 1 Costs LR 45

Compton (R) v Wiltshire Primary Care Trust
[2008] 6 Costs LR 898

Cope v United Dairies (London) Ltd
(1963) Costs LR (Core) 23

Cox and Carter v MGN Ltd and Others
[2006] 5 Costs LR 764

Crane v Canons Leisure Centre
[2008] 1 Costs LR 132

Crosbie v Munroe and Motor Insurers' Bureau
[2003] 3 Costs LR 377

Crouch v King's Healthcare NHS Trust; Murry v Blackburn Hyndburn & Ribble Valley Health Care NHS Trust
[2005] 2 Costs LR 200

Currey v Currey
[2007] 2 Costs LR 227

D Pride & Partners v Institute for Animal Health and Others
[2009] 5 Costs LR 803

Index of Reported Cases (1910–2009)

Daniels v London Borough of Lambeth
[1997] 1 Costs LR 64

Dart v Dart
[2002] 2 Costs LR 312

Davey v Aylesbury Vale District Council
[2007] 3 Costs LR 452

Davey v Aylesbury Vale District Council
[2008] 1 Costs LR 60

David Truex, Solicitor (a Firm) v Kitchin
[2007] 4 Costs LR 587

Davidsons (a Firm) v Jones-Fenleigh
(1980) Costs LR (Core) 70

Days Healthcare UK Ltd v Pihsiang Machinery Manufacturing Co Ltd and Others
[2006] 5 Costs LR 788

Dean & Dean Solicitors v Angel Airlines SA
[2007] 6 Costs LR 795

Dean & Dean v Angel Airlines SA
[2008] 6 Costs LR 866

Dempsey v Johnstone
[2004] 1 Costs LR 41

Designers Guild Ltd v Russell Williams (Textiles) Ltd
[2003] 2 Costs LR 204

Designers Guild Ltd v Russell Williams (Textiles) Ltd (t/a Washington DC)
[2003] 1 Costs LR 128

Dickinson (t/a John Dickinson Equipment Finance) v Rushmer (t/a F J Associates)
[2002] 1 Costs LR 128

Dolphin Quays Developments Ltd (in Administrative and Fixed Charge Receivership) v Mills and Others
[2008] 2 Costs LR 220

Douglas and Others v Hello! Ltd and Others
[2004] 2 Costs LR 304

Dymocks Franchise Systems (NSW) Pty Ltd v Todd and Others (No. 2)
[2005] 1 Costs LR 52

Dyson Technology Ltd v Strutt
[2007] 4 Costs LR 597

E C-L v DM
[2005] 4 Costs LR 576

Earles v Barclays Bank plc
[2009] 6 Costs LR 906

East Coast Aggregates Ltd and Para-Pagan and Others; Ross and (1) The Owners of the Ship "Bowbelle" (2) The Owners of the Ship "Marchioness"
[1997] 1 Costs LR 90

Eastwood (Deceased), Re, Lloyds Bank Ltd v Eastwood and Others
(1974) Costs LR (Core) 50

Easyair Ltd (t/a Openair) v Opal Telecom Ltd
[2009] 6 Costs LR 882

Electricity Supply Nominees Ltd v Farrell and Others
[1998] 1 Costs LR 49

Eversheds v Osman
[2000] 1 Costs LR 54

Index of Reported Cases (1910–2009)

Fattal and Fattal v Walbrook Trustees (Jersey) Ltd and Another
[2009] 4 Costs LR 591

Federal Bank of the Middle East v Hadkinson and Hadkinson and Others v Saab and Others
[2000] 1 Costs LR 94

Federation Against Copyright Theft (FACT) v Broomhall and Others
[2007] 4 Costs LR 640

Federation Against Copyright Theft (FACT) v North West Aerials and Others
[2006] 2 Costs LR 361

Fenton v Holmes
[2008] 2 Costs LR 238

Finley v Glaxo Laboratories Ltd
(1989) Costs LR (Core) 106

Fleming v Chief Constable of the Sussex Police Force
[2005] 1 Costs LR 1

Flynn v Scougall
[2005] 1 Costs LR 38

Forcelux Ltd v Binnie
[2009] 5 Costs LR 825

Fosberry v Her Majesty's Revenue & Customs
[2008] 3 Costs LR 380

Fosse Motor Engineers Ltd and Others v Conde Nast and National Magazine Distributors Ltd and Others
[2009] 3 Costs LR 377

Galandauer v Snaresbrook Crown Court
[2007] 2 Costs LR 205

Garbutt and Another v Edwards and Another
[2006] 1 Costs LR 143

Garrett v Halton Borough Council; Myatt and Others v National Coal Board
[2006] 5 Costs LR 798

Gaynor v Central West London Buses Ltd
[2007] 1 Costs LR 33

Gazley v Wade and News Group Newspapers Ltd
[2005] 1 Costs LR 129

General Mediterranean Holdings SA v Patel
[1999] 2 Costs LR 10

General of Berne Insurance Co (The) v Jardine Reinsurance Management Ltd and Others
[1997] 2 Costs LR 66

General of Berne Insurance Co v Jardine Reinsurance Management Ltd
[1998] 1 Costs LR 1

Geraghty & Co v Awwad and Another
[2000] 1 Costs LR 105

Giambrone and Others v JMC Holidays
[2002] 2 Costs LR 294

Giambrone and Others v JMC Holidays Ltd
[2003] 2 Costs LR 189

Gil v Baygreen Properties Ltd (in Liquidation) and Others
[2005] 1 Costs LR 75

Glossop v The Lord High Chancellor
[2005] 3 Costs LR 359

Index of Reported Cases (1910–2009)

Gloucestershire County Council v
    Evans and Others
    [2008] 2 Costs LR 308
Gold v Mincoff Science & Gold
    (a Firm)
    [2005] 1 Costs LR 30
Goldman v Hesper
    (1988) Costs LR (Core) 99
Goodman and Farr v The Secretary
    of State for Constitutional Affairs
    [2007] 3 Costs LR 366
Goodwood Recoveries Ltd v Breen;
    Breen v Slater
    [2007] 2 Costs LR 147
Gower Chemicals Group Litigation
    (Various Claimants in the) v
    Gower Chemicals Ltd and
    Another
    [2008] 4 Costs LR 582
Gray v Going Places Leisure
    Travel Ltd
    [2005] 3 Costs LR 405
Griffiths and Others v Solutia
    (UK) Ltd
    [2001] 1 Costs LR 99
Grupo Torras SA v Al-Sabah
    [2003] 2 Costs LR 294
Gundry v Sainsbury
    (1910) Costs LR (Core) 1

Haji-Ioannou and Others v Frangos
    and Others
    [2006] 2 Costs LR 315
Haji-Ioannou v Frangos and Others
    [2007] 2 Costs LR 253
Hall and Others v Stone
    [2008] 3 Costs LR 450

Hall v Rover Financial Services Ltd
    (GB) t/a Land Rover Financial
    Services
    [2003] 1 Costs LR 70
Hallam-Peel & Co v The Mayor
    and Burgesses of the London
    Borough of Southwark
    [2009] 2 Costs LR 269
Halloran v Delaney
    [2002] 3 Costs LR 503
Halsey v Milton Keynes General
    NHS Trust; Steel v Joy
    and Halliday
    [2004] 3 Costs LR 393
Harold v The Lord Chancellor
    [1999] 1 Costs LR 14
Harris and Hartless v Moat
    Housing Group-South Ltd
    [2008] 2 Costs LR 294
Harrison and Others v Tew
    (1990) Costs LR (Core) 124
Hart v Aga Khan Foundation (UK)
    (1984) Costs LR (Core) 87
Hatton v Hopkins and Another
    [2007] 2 Costs LR 172
Hawley v Luminar Leisure plc; ASE
    Security Services Ltd v Mann
    [2006] 5 Costs LR 687
Hazlett v Sefton Metropolitan
    Borough Council
    [2001] 1 Costs LR 89
Hedrich and Another v Standard
    Bank London Ltd
    [2008] 5 Costs LR 679
Henry v British Broadcasting
    Corporation
    [2006] 3 Costs LR 412

Index of Reported Cases (1910–2009)

Hickman v Blake Lapthorn and Fisher
[2006] 3 Costs LR 452

Higgs v Camden & Islington Health Authority
[2003] 2 Costs LR 211

Hill v Bailey
[2004] 1 Costs LR 135

Hinde v Harbourne and Others
[2004] 2 Costs LR 289

HLB Kidsons (a Firm) v Lloyds Underwriters
[2008] 3 Costs LR 427

HM Revenue & Customs v Viewtopia Ltd
[2006] 2 Costs LR 344

Hodgson and Others v Imperial Tobacco Ltd & Gallaher
[1998] 1 Costs LR 14

Hodgson and Others v Imperial Tobacco Ltd and Others (No. 2)
[1998] 2 Costs LR 27

Hollins v Russell and Related Appeals
[2003] 3 Costs LR 423

Holmes v Alfred McAlpine Homes (Yorkshire) Ltd
[2006] 3 Costs LR 466

Home Office v Lownds
[2002] 2 Costs LR 279

Homes Assured Corporation plc, In the Matter of: The Official Receiver v Dobson and Others and Sampson and Kohlbacher v Wilson and Others
[2002] 1 Costs LR 71

Hornsby and Others v Clark Kenneth Leventhal (a Firm) and Others
[2000] 2 Costs LR 295

Horsford v Bird and Others
[2007] 2 Costs LR 245

Howarth v Green
[2003] 2 Costs LR 160

HSS Hire Services Group plc v BMB Builders Merchants Ltd and Grafton Group (UK) plc
[2006] 2 Costs LR 213

Huck v Robson
[2003] 1 Costs LR 19

Hunt v East Dorset Health Authority
(1992) Costs LR (Core) 174

Hunt v R M Douglas (Roofing) Ltd
(1988) Costs LR (Core) 136

Hurst v Leeming
[2003] 2 Costs LR 153

Ikarian Reefer, The
[2000] 1 Costs LR 37

Ilangaratne v British Medical Association
[2006] 1 Costs LR 101

Ilangaratne v British Medical Association
[2008] 3 Costs LR 367

Inline Logistics Ltd v UCI Logistics Ltd
[2002] 2 Costs LR 304

Investment Invoice Financing Ltd v Limehouse Board Mills Ltd
[2006] 4 Costs LR 632

Irvine v Commissioner of Police for the Metropolis and Others
[2005] 3 Costs LR 380

Index of Reported Cases (1910–2009)

Irwin Mitchell v The Revenue and
  Customs Prosecutions Office
  and Allad
  [2009] 1 Costs LR 34

J Murphy & Sons Ltd v Johnston
  Precast Ltd (formerly Johnston
  Pipes Ltd) (No. 2 – Costs)
  [2009] 5 Costs LR 745
Jackson v The Lord Chancellor
  [2003] 3 Costs LR 395
Jefferson v National Freight
  Carriers plc
  [2001] 2 Costs LR 313
Jemma Trust Company Ltd v
  Liptrott and Others
  [2004] 1 Costs LR 66
Jemma Trust Company Ltd v
  Liptrott and Others (No. 2)
  [2004] 4 Costs LR 610
Jenkins v Young Brothers
  Transport Ltd
  [2006] 3 Costs LR 495
Johnson and Others v Reed
  Corrugated Cases Ltd
  (1990) Costs LR (Core) 180
Jonathan Alexander Ltd v Proctor
  (1995) Costs LR (Core) 399
Jones and Jones and Secretary of
  State for Wales and The Vale of
  Glamorgan Borough Council
  [1997] 1 Costs LR 34
Jones v Caradon Catnic Ltd
  [2006] 3 Costs LR 427
Jones v Wrexham Borough Council
  [2008] 1 Costs LR 147
Joseph v Boyd & Hutchinson
  [1999] 1 Costs LR 74

Kamenou & Another (t/a Regency
  Developments) v Pariser
  and Others
  [1999] 2 Costs LR 117
Kasir v Darlington & Simpson
  Rolling Mills Ltd
  [2001] 2 Costs LR 228
Kastor Navigation Co Ltd and
  Another v Axa Global Risks (UK)
  Ltd and Others;
  The "Kastor Too"
  [2004] 4 Costs LR 569
Kellar and Carib West Ltd
  v Williams
  [2005] 4 Costs LR 559
Kew v Bettamix Ltd and Others
  [2007] 4 Costs LR 527
Khan v Lord Chancellor
  [2003] 2 Costs LR 228
Kier Tankard v John Fredricks
  Plastics Ltd and Others
  [2009] 1 Costs LR 101
Kilby v Gawith
  [2008] 6 Costs LR 959
King v Telegraph Group Ltd
  [2004] 3 Costs LR 449
Kitchen v Burwell Reed
  & Kinghorn Ltd
  [2006] 1 Costs LR 82
Knight v Beyond Properties Pty Ltd
  and Others
  [2007] 1 Costs LR 5
Kostic v Chaplin and Others
  [2008] 2 Costs LR 271
Kris Motor Spares Ltd v Fox
  Williams LLP
  [2009] 6 Costs LR 931

Index of Reported Cases (1910–2009)

KU (a Child, By Her Mother and Litigation Friend PU) v Liverpool City Council
[2005] 4 Costs LR 600

Kundrath v Harry Kwatia & Gooding
[2005] 2 Costs LR 279

Kuwait Airways Corporation v Iraqi Airways Company (Body Corporate) and Others
[2003] 1 Costs LR 130

L v L
[1997] 1 Costs LR 9

Lahey v Pirelli Tyres Ltd
[2007] 3 Costs LR 462

Lamont v Burton
[2007] 4 Costs LR 574

Landau and Cohen v The Lord Chancellor's Department (R v Abraham)
[1999] 2 Costs LR 5

Latimer Management Consultants v Ellingham Investments Ltd (Mr Peires)
[2008] 1 Costs LR 1

Laurence and Laurence v Singh (t/a K & T Investments)
[1997] 1 Costs LR 58

Law Society v Persaud
(1990) Costs LR (Core) 114

Lay and Others v Drexler and Others
[2007] 5 Costs LR 695

Ledward Claimants v Kent & Medway Health Authority and East Kent Hospitals NHS Trust; Cost Capping Application
[2004] 1 Costs LR 101

Leeds City Council v Carr and Coles & Wells v Barnsley Metropolitan Borough Council
[2000] 1 Costs LR 144

Legal Services Commission v Rasool
[2008] 4 Costs LR 529

Leigh v Michelin Tyre plc
[2004] 1 Costs LR 148

Leopold Lazarus Ltd v Secretary of State for Trade and Industry
(1976) Costs LR (Core) 62

Less and Others v Benedict
[2005] 4 Costs LR 688

Lifeline Gloves Ltd v Richardson and Richardson
[2006] 1 Costs LR 58

Liverpool Freeport Electronics Ltd and Others v Habib Bank Ltd and The Legal Services Commission
[2009] 3 Costs LR 434

Lloyds TSB Bank plc v Lampert
[2003] 2 Costs LR 286

Lobster Group Ltd v Heidelberg Graphic Equipment Ltd and Another
[2008] 5 Costs LR 724

Locabail (UK) Ltd v Bayfield Properties and Others and Emmanuel v Locabail (UK) Ltd and Another
[2000] 2 Costs LR 169

London Borough of "A" v M and SF
(1994) Costs LR (Core) 374

London Borough of Enfield v P
[1997] 1 Costs LR 73

Index of Reported Cases (1910–2009)

London Borough of Southwark v
Nejad and Others
[1999] 1 Costs LR 62

Lord Chancellor (The) v John
Charles Rees QC and Others
[2009] 2 Costs LR 334

Lord Chancellor v Frieze
[2007] 5 Costs LR 684

Lord Chancellor v Haggan
and Others
[2007] 5 Costs LR 722

Lord Chancellor v Singh
[2003] 1 Costs LR 62

Lord Chancellor v Taylor
[2000] 1 Costs LR 1

Loveday v Renton and Another
(No. 2)
(1991) Costs LR (Core) 204

Lownds v Home Office
[2002] 2 Costs LR 279

Lynch v Paul Davidson Taylor
(a Firm)
[2004] 2 Costs LR 321

Macdonald v Taree Holdings
[2001] 1 Costs LR 147

Macdougall v Boote Edgar Esterkin
(a Firm)
[2001] 1 Costs LR 118

MacPherson v Bevan Ashford
[2003] 3 Costs LR 389

Macro (Ipswich) Ltd, In re
[1997] 1 Costs LR 128

Maes Finance Ltd v WG Edwards &
Partners
[2000] 2 Costs LR 198

Mainwaring and Lisle and Goldtech
Investments Ltd; Goldtech
Investments Ltd and Mainwaring
and Lisle
[1997] 1 Costs LR 143

Mainwaring and Lisle v Goldtech
Investments Ltd
[1999] 1 Costs LR 96

Malkinson v Trim
[2002] 3 Costs LR 515

Malmesbury (James Carleton,
Seventh Earl of Malmesbury) and
Others v Strutt & Parker
(a Partnership)
[2008] 5 Costs LR 736

Maltby and Another v D J Freeman
& Co (a Firm)
(1977) Costs LR (Core) 64

Mamidoil – Jetoil Greek Petroleum
Company SA and Moil – Coal
Trading Company Ltd v Okta
Crude Oil Refinery AD
[2003] 2 Costs LR 175

Manches LLP v Green; Green v
Manches LLP and the Former
Partners in Marshall Ross &
Prevezer (a Firm)
[2008] 6 Costs LR 881

Mars UK Ltd v
Teknowledge Ltd
[1999] 2 Costs LR 44

Martin v Holland and Barrett
[2002] 3 Costs LR 530

Mastercigars Direct Ltd v Withers
LLP
[2008] 1 Costs LR 72

MasterCigars Direct Ltd v Withers
LLP
[2009] 3 Costs LR 393

Index of Reported Cases (1910–2009)

McGlinn v Waltham Contractors Ltd and Others
[2006] 1 Costs LR 27
McIlwraith v McIlwraith
[2004] 4 Costs LR 533
McLinden v Redbond
[2006] 4 Costs LR 651
McPherson v BNP Paribas (London Branch)
[2004] 4 Costs LR 596
McPhilemy v Times Newspapers Ltd and Others (No. 4)
[2001] 2 Costs LR 295
Mealing-McLeod v The Common Professional Examination Board
[2000] 2 Costs LR 223
Medcalf v Mardell
[2002] 3 Costs LR 428
Medway Oil and Storage Co Ltd v Continental Contractors Ltd and Others
(1928) Costs LR (Core) 5
Meeke and Taylor v Secretary of State for Constitutional Affairs
[2006] 1 Costs LR 1
Meretz Investments NV and Britel Corporation NV v ACP Ltd and Others
[2008] 1 Costs LR 42
Metalloy Supplies Ltd v MA (UK) Ltd
[1998] 1 Costs LR 85
Michaelides, Re
[2005] 2 Costs LR 191
Miller Gardner v The Lord Chancellor
[1997] 2 Costs LR 29
Miller v Hales and Others
[2007] 4 Costs LR 521

Mills v Birchall and Gilbertson
[2008] 4 Costs LR 599
MMR/MR Vaccine Litigation; Afrika and Others v Cape plc; X, Y, Z and Others v Schering Health Care Ltd; Sayers and Others v Merck and Smithkline Beecham plc
[2003] 4 Costs LR 503
Mohammadi v Shellpoint Trustees Ltd and Anston Investments Ltd
[2009] 3 Costs LR 486
Mohammed v Alaga & Co
[1999] 2 Costs LR 169
Montlake and Others (as Trustees of Wasps Football Club) v Lambert Smith Hampton Group Ltd
[2004] 4 Costs LR 650
Moon v Garrett and Others
[2007] 1 Costs LR 41
Morgan and Others v Legal Aid Board
[2001] 1 Costs LR 57
Morgan v UPS
[2009] 3 Costs LR 384
Morris v Lord Chancellor
[2000] 1 Costs LR 88
Morris v Wiltshire and Woodspring District Council and the Supreme Court Costs Office
[2002] 1 Costs LR 167
Mount Cook Land Ltd and Another (R) v Westminster City Council
[2004] 2 Costs LR 211
Mullings v (1) Boahemaah (2) Kudum-Bradley (3) Toppin
[1998] 1 Costs LR 57

Index of Reported Cases (1910–2009)

Multiplex Constructions (UK) Ltd v Cleveland Bridge UK Ltd and Another (No. 7)
[2009] 1 Costs LR 55

Murphy and Another v Young & Co's Brewery and Another
[1998] 1 Costs LR 94

Murria v Lord Chancellor
[2000] 1 Costs LR 81

Myatt and Others v National Coal Board
[2007] 4 Costs LR 564

Myler and Mirror Group Newspapers v Williams
[2003] 4 Costs LR 566

National Westminster Bank plc v Rabobank Nederland
[2008] 3 Costs LR 396

National Westminster Bank plc v Rabobank Nederland (No. 3)
[2008] 6 Costs LR 839

Nederlandse Reassurantie Groep Holding NV v (1) Bacon and Woodrow (a Firm) (2) Ernst and Young (a Firm) (3) Swiss Bank Corp (4–47,45–59) Anderton and Others
[1998] 2 Costs LR 32

Nedlloyd Lines UK Ltd and Another v CEL Group Ltd
[2004] 2 Costs LR 286

Newall v Lewis and Others
[2008] 4 Costs LR 626

Nicholas Drukker & Co v Pridie Brewster & Co
[2006] 3 Costs LR 439

Norris v Norris; Haskins v Haskins
[2003] 4 Costs LR 591

Northstar Systems Ltd and Others v Fielding and Others
[2007] 2 Costs LR 264

Nossen's Patent, Re
(1968) Costs LR (Core) 36

Nugent and Killick v Michael Goss Aviation and Others
[2002] 3 Costs LR 359

Nykredit Mortgage Bank plc v Edward Erdman Group Ltd (formerly Edward Erdman (an Unlimited Company)) (No. 2)
[1998] 1 Costs LR 108

Official Receiver (The) v Brunt and Others
[1998] 2 Costs LR 38

Official Receiver (The) v Brunt and Others
[1999] 2 Costs LR 97

Oliver v Whipps Cross University Hospital NHS Trust and Waltham Forest Primary Care Trust
[2009] 3 Costs LR 474

Ortwein v Rugby Mansions Ltd
[2004] 1 Costs LR 26

Painting v University of Oxford
[2005] 3 Costs LR 394

Palmer v The Estate of Kevin Palmer (Deceased) and Others
[2008] 4 Costs LR 513

Paragon Finance plc v Noueiri
[2002] 1 Costs LR 12

Patten (t/a Anthony Patten & Co) v Lord Chancellor
[2001] 2 Costs LR 233

Index of Reported Cases (1910–2009)

Paturel v Marble Arch Services Ltd
[2006] 4 Costs LR 556
Pauls Agriculture Ltd v Smith and Others
(1992) Costs LR (Core) 218
Peacock v MGN Ltd
[2009] 4 Costs LR 584
Pearce v Ove Arup Partnership Ltd and Others
[2004] 4 Costs LR 631
Persaud v Persaud and Others
[2004] 1 Costs LR 1
Petromec Inc v Petroleo Brasileiro SA Petrobras
[2007] 2 Costs LR 212
Petrotrade Inc v Texaco Ltd
[2002] 1 Costs LR 60
Phillips and Others v Symes (a Bankrupt) and Others; in the matter of an issue ordered to be tried between: Symes (a Bankrupt) v Phillips and Others
[2005] 2 Costs LR 224
Pilbrow v Pearless de Rougemont & Co
[1999] 2 Costs LR 109
Pine v The Law Society
[2002] 3 Costs LR 347
Piper Double Glazing Ltd v DC Contracts
(1992) Costs LR (Core) 256
Platt v GKN Kwikform Ltd
(1992) Costs LR (Core) 250
Plender v Hyams
[2001] 1 Costs LR 109
Powell v Herefordshire Health Authority
[2003] 2 Costs LR 185
PR Records Ltd v Vinyl 2000 Ltd and Owlett (Susan) and Owlett (Adrian)
[2008] 1 Costs LR 19
Pritchard v Ford Motor Co Ltd; Riccio v Ford Motor Co Ltd
[1997] 1 Costs LR 39
Property and Reversionary Investment Corporation Ltd v Secretary of State for the Environment
(1975) Costs LR (Core) 54

R (Brewer) v Supreme Court Costs Office
[2007] 1 Costs LR 20
R (Buglife – The Invertebrate Conservation Trust) v Thurrock Thames Gateway Development Corp and Another
[2009] 1 Costs LR 80
R (Bullmore) v West Hertfordshire Hospitals NHS Trust
[2007] 6 Costs LR 844
R (Corner House Research) v The Secretary of State for Trade and Industry
[2005] 3 Costs LR 455
R (Davies) (No. 2) v HM Deputy Coroner for Birmingham
[2004] 4 Costs LR 545
R (E) v Governing Body of JFS and Others
[2009] 4 Costs LR 695
R (Factortame and Others) v Secretary of State for Transport
[2002] 3 Costs LR 467

Index of Reported Cases (1910–2009)

R (Roudham and Larling Parish
    Council) v Breckland Council
    and Paul Rackham Ltd
    (Interested Party)
  [2009] 2 Costs LR 282
R (Spiteri) v Basildon Crown Court
  [2009] 5 Costs LR 772
R (Wulfsohn) v Legal Services
    Commission
  [2002] 3 Costs LR 341
R v Agbobu
  [2009] 2 Costs LR 374
R v Ainsworth
  [2007] 6 Costs LR 865
R v Alays and Others
  [2007] 2 Costs LR 321
R v Al-Goni and Ataya
  [2009] 2 Costs LR 356
R v Ali and Others
  (1984) Costs LR (Core) 434
R v Alwan
  [2000] 2 Costs LR 326
R v Amin
  [2009] 1 Costs LR 149
R v Armstrong
  [2008] 5 Costs LR 794
R v Austin
  [2006] 5 Costs LR 857
R v Ayres
  [2002] 2 Costs LR 330
R v Backhouse
  (1986) Costs LR (Core) 445
R v Baker and Fowler
  [2004] 4 Costs LR 693
R v Balme
  [2008] 6 Costs LR 988
R v Bell
  [2003] 1 Costs LR 144

R v Bellas and five other appeals
  (1986) Costs LR (Core) 479
R v Bhatti
  [2006] 2 Costs LR 356
R v Bishop
  [2008] 5 Costs LR 808
R v Bishop and Others
  [2007] 3 Costs LR 506
R v Bolton
  [2006] 4 Costs LR 659
R v Bolton (Stephen George)
  [2005] 2 Costs LR 334
R v Bond (Michael)
  [2005] 3 Costs LR 532
R v Boswell; R v Halliwell
  (1987) Costs LR (Core) 507
R v Bowles
  [2007] 3 Costs LR 514
R v Bowman
  [2007] 1 Costs LR 1
R v Brewer
  [2007] 4 Costs LR 662
R v Briers (Michael)
  [2005] 1 Costs LR 146
R v Brinkworth
  [2006] 3 Costs LR 512
R v Brook
  [2004] 1 Costs LR 178
R v Brown
  [2002] 3 Costs LR 539
R v Cadogan
  [2009] 5 Costs LR 853
R v Carlyle
  [2002] 1 Costs LR 192
R v Carty
  [2009] 3 Costs LR 500
R v Cevik
  [1998] 2 Costs LR 1

Index of Reported Cases (1910–2009)

R v Chapple
 [2007] 2 Costs LR 310
R v Cheng
 [2008] 1 Costs LR 180
R v Cheng and Chen
 [2007] 4 Costs LR 626
R v Cheng, Chen and Miah
 [2007] 4 Costs LR 634
R v Chowdhury
 [2009] 3 Costs LR 514
R v Chubb
 [2002] 2 Costs LR 333
R v Clarke
 (1991) Costs LR (Core) 496
R v Comer
 [2009] 6 Costs LR 972
R v Conboy
 (1990) Costs LR (Core) 493
R v Conroy
 [2004] 1 Costs LR 182
R v Coutts (Graham)
 [2007] 6 Costs LR 878
R v Cowie
 [2006] 2 Costs LR 375
R v Crocker
 [2001] 1 Costs LR 25
R v Crucefix
 [2007] 5 Costs LR 770
R v Dalziell
 [2003] 4 Costs LR 651
R v Davies
 (1985) Costs LR (Core) 472
R v Davies
 [2008] 5 Costs LR 813
R v Davies (Benjamin)
 [2007] 1 Costs LR 116
R v Dawson
 [1999] 1 Costs LR 4

R v Despres
 [2005] 4 Costs LR 750
R v Dhaliwal
 [2004] 4 Costs LR 689
R v Dhesi
 [2003] 4 Costs LR 645
R v Dodd and Ward
 [2009] 2 Costs LR 368
R v Dunlop
 [2008] 5 Costs LR 803
R v Duxbury
 (1983) Costs LR (Core) 423
R v Duzgun and Another
 [2000] 2 Costs LR 316
R v Edwards
 [2004] 4 Costs LR 679
R v Evans-Southall and Others
 [1998] 1 Costs LR 68
R v Fairhurst
 [2000] 1 Costs LR 34
R v Farrell and Selby
 [2007] 3 Costs LR 495
R v Faulkner
 [2003] 1 Costs LR 148
R v Faulkner and Others
 [1998] 1 Costs LR 66
R v Findlay and McGregor
 [2002] 2 Costs LR 322
R v Finn
 [2006] 3 Costs LR 525
R v Foot
 [2004] 3 Costs LR 525
R v Ford-Lloyd
 (1984) Costs LR (Core) 424
R v Frampton
 [2005] 3 Costs LR 527
R v Franks
 [2008] 5 Costs LR 819

Index of Reported Cases (1910–2009)

R v Ghadhim Gerhards
(1984) Costs LR (Core) 463
R v Ghaffar
[2009] 6 Costs LR 980
R v Gill (Steven)
[2006] 5 Costs LR 837
R v Gittins and Khan
[2007] 4 Costs LR 549
R v Goodwin
(1984) Costs LR (Core) 425
R v Goodwin
[2008] 3 Costs LR 497
R v Grant
[2006] 1 Costs LR 173
R v Gray (Richard)
[2009] 6 Costs LR 967
R v Great Western Trains Company Ltd
[2004] 2 Costs LR 331
R v Griffin
[2008] 3 Costs LR 483
R v Hadley
[2005] 3 Costs LR 548
R v Halcrow
(1984) Costs LR (Core) 436
R v Hameed
[2001] 2 Costs LR 343
R v Hann
[2009] 5 Costs LR 833
R v Hardev Singh
[2002] 1 Costs LR 196
R v Harper
[2007] 6 Costs LR 862
R v Harris
[2009] 3 Costs LR 507
R v Hashash
[2008] 4 Costs LR 646
R v Hayes
[2008] 1 Costs LR 186

R v Hendy-Freegard
[2007] 5 Costs LR 776
R v Henshaw
[2006] 1 Costs LR 191
R v Hill and Dalton
[2007] 5 Costs LR 788
R v Hindle
(1987) Costs LR (Core) 486
R v Hudson
(1985) Costs LR (Core) 456
R v Huggett
(1988) Costs LR (Core) 488
R v Hussain and Others
(1984) Costs LR (Core) 426
R v Islami
[2009] 6 Costs LR 988
R v Ismail
[2006] 3 Costs LR 530
R v Johnson
[2006] 5 Costs LR 852
R v Johnson
[2008] 6 Costs LR 983
R v Johnson (Craig)
[2007] 2 Costs LR 316
R v Johnson (L)
[2005] 1 Costs LR 153
R v Johnson and 13 Others
[2008] 2 Costs LR 337
R v Johnson and 13 Others
[2009] 4 Costs LR 710
R v Jones (John Ivor)
[2007] 6 Costs LR 873
R v Judd
[2006] 2 Costs LR 340
R v K, G and M
[2005] 4 Costs LR 571
R v Kayani
[2007] 3 Costs LR 490

Index of Reported Cases (1910–2009)

R v Kelly and Others
 [2004] 2 Costs LR 344
R v Kennedy (Francis)
 [2006] 4 Costs LR 662
R v Khair (Lee)
 [2005] 3 Costs LR 542
R v Khan (Zulfi Al)
 [2003] 1 Costs LR 137
R v Knight
 [2003] 3 Costs LR 496
R v Larsh
 [2007] 5 Costs LR 783
R v Lawrence
 [2000] 2 Costs LR 334
R v Lawrence
 [2007] 1 Costs LR 138
R v Leigh (John)
 [2008] 1 Costs LR 191
R v Long
 [2009] 1 Costs LR 151
R v Maguire
 [2006] 4 Costs LR 678
R v Mahmood
 [2008] 2 Costs LR 326
R v Mahon
 [1999] 2 Costs LR 151
R v Marandola
 [2006] 1 Costs LR 184
R v Martin
 [2004] 1 Costs LR 167
R v Martin and Others
 [2007] 1 Costs LR 128
R v Mashhour
 [2003] 2 Costs LR 318
R v Matthews (Rosalind) and Others
 [2007] 2 Costs LR 328
R v McClean
 [2005] 4 Costs LR 740

R v McGunigle (Thomas)
 [2005] 3 Costs LR 537
R v Miller
 (1984) Costs LR (Core) 431
R v Mills and Morris
 (1993) Costs LR (Core) 498
R v Mold Crown Court ex parte Khan
 [2001] 2 Costs LR 336
R v Moss
 (1984) Costs LR (Core) 437
R v Neil and five other appeals
 (1986) Costs LR (Core) 475
R v Newport
 [2009] 6 Costs LR 983
R v O'Brien
 (1985) Costs LR (Core) 440
R v O'Brien
 [2003] 4 Costs LR 625
R v O'Brien and Ollife
 (1984) Costs LR (Core) 505
R v Oates
 [2002] 3 Costs LR 375
R v Oldcorn
 [2003] 2 Costs LR 310
R v Ortiz-Ortega
 [2008] 6 Costs LR 976
R v Osagie
 (1984) Costs LR (Core) 433
R v Ozen
 [2006] 5 Costs LR 847
R v Panice
 (1984) Costs LR (Core) 462
R v Phillips
 [2007] 1 Costs LR 121
R v Phillips
 [2009] 6 Costs LR 993
R v Pickett
 [2004] 3 Costs LR 529

Index of Reported Cases (1910–2009)

R v Pitchforth and Brighouse (CPS Appeal)
[2005] 4 Costs LR 721
R v Plews
(1984) Costs LR (Core) 466
R v Prenga
[2004] 4 Costs LR 699
R v Preston Crown Court ex parte Lancashire County Council
[1999] 1 Costs LR 58
R v Pullum
(1983) Costs LR (Core) 413
R v Raji
[2003] 4 Costs LR 636
R v Ranjit
[2006] 3 Costs LR 541
R v Richardson
[2008] 2 Costs LR 320
R v Rigelsford
[2006] 3 Costs LR 518
R v Roberts
[2008] 2 Costs LR 323
R v Rose
[2008] 1 Costs LR 198
R v Russell
[2008] 3 Costs LR 501
R v Russell (Sebastian Lee)
[2006] 5 Costs LR 841
R v Rycott
(1992) Costs LR (Core) 449
R v Sandhu
(1984) Costs LR (Core) 451
R v Sanghera and Others
[2008] 5 Costs LR 823
R v Secretary of State for the Home Department ex parte Gunn
[2001] 2 Costs LR 263
R v Shacklady (Andrew)
[2005] 4 Costs LR 716
R v Shaw (Mark Anthony)
[2005] 2 Costs LR 326
R v Slessor
(1984) Costs LR (Core) 438
R v Smith
[2004] 2 Costs LR 348
R v Smith (Philip)
[2008] 4 Costs LR 656
R v Smith (Thomas)
[2006] 1 Costs LR 167
R v Solomka
[2007] 6 Costs LR 868
R v Sood
[2004] 3 Costs LR 520
R v Staniland (Craig)
[2005] 2 Costs LR 337
R v Starr
[2009] 5 Costs LR 841
R v Stewart
[2004] 3 Costs LR 501
R v Sturdy
[1999] 1 Costs LR 1
R v Sturmer and Lewis
[2009] 2 Costs LR 364
R v Sullivan
(1989) Costs LR (Core) 490
R v Supreme Court Taxing Office ex parte John Singh and Co
[1997] 1 Costs LR 49
R v Syed
[2004] 4 Costs LR 686
R v Tanimowo
[2008] 2 Costs LR 331
R v Taylor
[2000] 1 Costs LR 32
R v Taylor
[2005] 4 Costs LR 712
R v Theobald
[2008] 4 Costs LR 662

Index of Reported Cases (1910–2009)

R v Thomas; R v Davidson; R v Hutton
(1985) Costs LR (Core) 469
R v Thompson
[2006] 4 Costs LR 668
R v Tooth (David Christopher) (CPS Appeal)
[2007] 2 Costs LR 302
R v Tucker
[2009] 5 Costs LR 850
R v Villiers
[2005] 4 Costs LR 732
R v Wallace
[2008] 3 Costs LR 494
R v Walpole
[2002] 1 Costs LR 199
R v Wanklyn
(1985) Costs LR (Core) 443
R v Ward-Allen
[2005] 4 Costs LR 745
R v Warren
[2006] 2 Costs LR 336
R v Wellman and Others
[2009] 1 Costs LR 137
R v White
[2008] 3 Costs LR 479
R v Winskill
[2008] 4 Costs LR 651
R v Zemb
(1985) Costs LR (Core) 442
Rackham v Sandy and Others
[2006] 1 Costs LR 34
Radu v Houston and Another
[2007] 5 Costs LR 671
Ralph Hume Garry (a Firm) v Gwillim
[2003] 1 Costs LR 77
Read v Edmed
[2006] 2 Costs LR 201

Reed Executive plc and Reed Solutions plc v Reed Business Information Ltd, Reed Elsevier (UK) Ltd and Totaljobs.com Ltd
[2004] 4 Costs LR 662
Reeves v Sprecher and Others
[2009] 1 Costs LR 1
Reid Minty (a Firm) v Taylor
[2002] 1 Costs LR 180
Reid v The Capita Group plc
[2006] 4 Costs LR 564
Report from the Appeal Committee of the House of Lords
[2000] 1 Costs LR 7
Reynolds v Stone Rowe Brewer (a Firm)
[2008] 4 Costs LR 545
Rezvi and Rezvi v Brown Cooper (a Firm)
[1997] 1 Costs LR 109
Richard Buxton (Solicitors) v Mills-Owens
[2008] 6 Costs LR 948
Richards & Wallington (Plant Hire) Ltd v Monk & Co Ltd
(1984) Costs LR (Core) 79
Richardson Roofing Company Ltd v Ballast plc (Dissolved) and Others
[2009] 1 Costs LR 14
Richardson Roofing Company Ltd v The Colman Partnership Ltd
[2009] 4 Costs LR 521
Ridehalgh v Horsefield and Another
(1994) Costs LR (Core) 268
Riniker v University College London
[2001] 1 Costs LR 20

Index of Reported Cases (1910–2009)

RM Broudie & Co v
 The Lord Chancellor
 [2000] 2 Costs LR 285
Roach and Roach v The Home
 Office; Matthews v
 The Home Office
 [2009] 2 Costs LR 287
Rogers v Merthyr Tydfil County
 Borough Council
 [2007] 1 Costs LR 77
Rosling King v Rothschild Trust
 [2005] 2 Costs LR 165
Ross v Bowbelle (Owners)
 and Another
 [1998] 1 Costs LR 32
Ross v Stonewood Securities Ltd
 [2005] 1 Costs LR 89
Roundstone Nurseries Ltd v
 Stephenson Holdings Ltd
 [2009] 5 Costs LR 787
Royal Bank of Scotland v Allianz
 International Insurance Co
 and Others
 (1994) Costs LR (Core) 344
Russell Young & Co v Brown
 and Others
 [2007] 4 Costs LR 552
Ruttle Plant Hire Ltd v Department
 For Environment, Food &
 Rural Affairs
 [2007] 5 Costs LR 750

Sarwar v Alam
 [2002] 1 Costs LR 37
Scribes West Ltd v Relsa Anstalt and
 Another (No. 1)
 [2005] 1 Costs LR 18
Seaga v Harper
 [2009] 4 Costs LR 607

Secretary of State for Constitutional
 Affairs v Stork
 [2006] 1 Costs LR 69
Serious Organised Crime Agency v
 Szepietowski and Others
 [2009] 4 Costs LR 532
Serious Organised Crime Agency v
 Szepietowski and Others
 [2009] 4 Costs LR 615
SES Contracting Ltd and Others v
 UK Coal plc
 [2007] 5 Costs LR 758
Sharratt and Others and Rowe
 Cohen (a Firm) v London Central
 Bus Company Ltd and Others
 [2006] 4 Costs LR 584
Shepherds Investments Ltd v Walters
 and Others
 [2007] 6 Costs LR 837
Sheppard v Essex Strategic Health
 Authority
 [2006] 1 Costs LR 8
Shirley v Caswell
 [2001] 1 Costs LR 1
Sibley & Co v Reachbyte Ltd and
 Kris Motor Spares Ltd
 [2009] 2 Costs LR 311
Simms and Others v The Law
 Society
 [2006] 2 Costs LR 245
Simpson v Bowker
 [2007] 6 Costs LR 850
Simpsons Motor Sales (London) Ltd
 v Hendon Corporation (No. 2)
 (1964) Costs LR (Core) 29
Sims v Hawkins
 [2008] 5 Costs LR 691

Index of Reported Cases (1910–2009)

Sinclair (in His Capacity as the Former Receiver) v Glatt and Others
[2009] 4 Costs LR 568

Sinclair v British Telecommunications plc
[2001] 1 Costs LR 40

Sisu Capital Fund Ltd and Others v Tucker and Others
[2006] 2 Costs LR 262

Skuse v Granada Television Ltd
(1993) Costs LR (Core) 333

Slatter v Ronaldsons
[2002] 2 Costs LR 267

Smart v East Cheshire NHS Trust
[2004] 1 Costs LR 124

Smith Graham v The Lord Chancellor's Department (R v Carr)
[1999] 2 Costs LR 1

Smithkline Beecham plc and Glaxosmithkline UK Ltd v Apotex Europe Ltd and Others; Apotex Europe Ltd and Others v Beecham Group plc and Smithkline Beecham plc
[2005] 2 Costs LR 293

Smiths Dock Ltd v Edwards and Others
[2004] 3 Costs LR 440

Snowden v Ministry of Defence
[2002] 2 Costs LR 249

Solutia UK Ltd v Griffiths and 165 Others
[2001] 2 Costs LR 247

Sony Music Entertainment Inc and Sony Music Entertainment (UK) Ltd v Prestige Records Ltd and Dancebuy Ltd (t/a Slam Music)
[2000] 2 Costs LR 186

South Coast Shipping Company Ltd v Havant Borough Council
[2002] 1 Costs LR 98

Spath Holme Ltd v Chairman of the Greater Manchester and Lancashire Rent Assessment Committee and Others; Curtis v Chairman of the London Rent Assessment Committee & Another
[1998] 1 Costs LR 40

Spencer v Wood and Wood t/a Gordons Tyres (a Firm)
[2004] 3 Costs LR 372

Stacy v Player
[2004] 4 Costs LR 585

Sterling Publications v Burroughs
[2000] 2 Costs LR 155

Strachey v Ramage
[2009] 1 Costs LR 9

Straker v Tudor Rose (a Firm)
[2008] 2 Costs LR 205

Strydom v Vendside Ltd
[2009] 6 Costs LR 886

Stubblefield and Others v Kemp and Others
[2001] 1 Costs LR 30

Stubbs v Board of Governors of the Royal National Orthopaedic Hospital
(1988) Costs LR (Core) 117

Index of Reported Cases (1910–2009)

Suisse Security Bank and Trust Ltd v Governor of the Central Bank of the Bahamas (The Bahamas) [2007] 2 Costs LR 222

Sullivan v The Co-Operative Insurance Society Ltd [1999] 2 Costs LR 158

Supperstone v Hurst and Hurst [2008] 4 Costs LR 572

Sutton v Horsham District Council [2005] 2 Costs LR 344

Symes v Phillips and Others [2006] 4 Costs LR 553

Symphony Group plc v Hodgson (1993) Costs LR (Core) 319

Szekeres v Alan Smeath & Co [2005] 4 Costs LR 707

Tanfern Ltd v Cameron-Macdonald [2000] 2 Costs LR 260

Thai Trading Co (a Firm) v Taylor [1998] 1 Costs LR 122

The Accident Group Test Cases: Sharratt v London Central Bus Company and Other Cases [2004] 3 Costs LR 422

Thomas Joyce v Kammac Ltd (1988) Costs LR (Core) 353

Thomas v Bunn, etc (1990) Costs LR (Core) 161

Thomas Watts & Co (a Firm) v Smith [1998] 2 Costs LR 59

Thomson v Berkhamsted Collegiate School and Others [2009] 6 Costs LR 859

Thornley v Lang [2004] 1 Costs LR 91

Three Rivers District Council and Others v The Governor and Company of the Bank of England [2006] 5 Costs LR 714

Tierney v News Group Newspapers Ltd [2006] 4 Costs LR 606

Treasury Solicitor v Regester and Another (1977) Costs LR (Core) 42

Truex v Toll [2009] 5 Costs LR 758

Truscott v Truscott; Wraith v Sheffield Forgemasters Ltd [1997] 2 Costs LR 74

Trustees of Stokes Pension Fund v Western Power Distribution (South West) plc [2006] 2 Costs LR 226

Turner & Co v O Palomo SA [1999] 2 Costs LR 184

University of East London Higher Education Corporation v London Borough of Barking and Dagenham and Others (No. 2) [2005] 2 Costs LR 287

Utaniko Ltd v P&O Nedlloyd BV; East West Corp v Dampskibsselskabet AF, 1912 Aktieselskab and Another [2003] 4 Costs LR 531

Utting v McBain [2008] 3 Costs LR 442

Various Claimants v Gower Chemicals Ltd and Others [2007] 4 Costs LR 647

Index of Reported Cases (1910–2009)

Various Ledward Claimants v Kent
& Medway Health Authority and
East Kent Hospitals NHS Trust;
Cost Capping Application
[2004] 1 Costs LR 101

Venture Finance plc v Mead
and Another
[2006] 3 Costs LR 389

W (a Child), Re; D and DW v
Portsmouth Hospital NHS Trust
[2006] 5 Costs LR 742

Wagstaff v Colls
[2003] 4 Costs LR 535

Wakeling v Harrington (Liquidator
of Chelmsford City Football Club
(1980) Ltd)
[2007] 5 Costs LR 710

Walker v Walker
[2005] 3 Costs LR 363

Wallace and Wallace v Brian Gale
& Associates
[1997] 2 Costs LR 15

Wallace and Wallace v Brian Gale
& Associates (a Firm)
[1998] 2 Costs LR 53

Waterson Hicks v Eliopoulos
and Others
(1995) Costs LR (Core) 363

Weaver v London Quadrant
Housing Trust
[2009] 6 Costs LR 875

Westland Helicopters Ltd v Sheikh
Salah Al-Hejailan
[2006] 4 Costs LR 549

Westminster City Council v Porter
and Weeks; Citroen Wells (a
Firm) and Chorles (Respondents)
[2005] 2 Costs LR 186

Wills and Others v The Crown
Estate Commissioners and Others
[2003] 4 Costs LR 581

Wilson v The Specter Partnership
and Others
[2007] 6 Costs LR 802

Wilson v William Sturges & Co
(a Firm)
[2006] 4 Costs LR 614

Wong v Vizards
[1997] 2 Costs LR 46

Wraith and Sheffield
Forgemasters Ltd
[1997] 1 Costs LR 23

Young v JR Smart (Builders) Ltd
[2004] 2 Costs LR 298